David Bowie:

"I was in this plane over America when we ran into a heavy storm. I've never been so scared in my life. The plane was thrown about and I just gripped my seat and prayed and prayed. It was horrible! I've tried to use boats and trains as much as possible ever since!"

Joe Jackson:

"My worst moment was falling over on stage and breaking my ankle. I had to do a whole tour with my leg in plaster sitting on stage on a stool! It was real torture because I kept wanting to leap around and act as mad as usual — but every time I tried, I just fell down and the band had to pick me up and prop me back on the stupid stool!"

Michael Jackson:

"I've had plenty of hairy times in planes, but the worst for me was on the ground! It was at an airport. I was trying to escape from hundreds of chasing fans to get to the aeroplane which was waiting on the runway.

"Everyone was yelling to me to hurry up when I suddenly tripped and fell flat. The fans were getting closer all the time and I was convinced that, although they were only being friendly, I'd probably be shredded if they reached me. I just managed to get up and reach the plane in time!"

Kate Garner, Haysi Fantayzee:

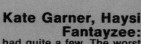

"I've had quite a few. The worst was probably when I was a member of a religious group and they wouldn't allow me to leave the house for months. I wanted to escape but I couldn't. Another horrible moment was being attacked when I was travelling to India. It was in Turkey and it scared the wits out of me!"

Nick Beggs, Kajagoogoo:

"I'm a real animal lover and my worst moment happened when I was working as a bin man.

"I was just about to put a bag of garbage into the machine when I heard a noise. There at the bottom of the bag was a lovely little gerbil.

"Great, you might think, I'd just saved it from a horrible death — but then the lady who owned it saw what was happening and said since I'd saved it, she might as well keep it, and demanded it back. Although I wanted to look after it myself I had to hand it over to someone who obviously didn't care one bit about it. Honestly, people like that shouldn't be allowed *near* animals!"

£2·10

CONTENTS

Welcome to this year's Jackie Annual — it's better than ever! There's so much in it for you to enjoy — great photo stories, eye-catching fashion, unbeatable beauty and lots of pop! There's loads to read, too — we've some great stories and readers' true experiences, long looks at what the stars forecast for you and fun quizzes that'll give you a giggle. You can't beat this year's Jackie Annual — it's g-g-g-great! Hope you enjoy it, and remember, we're around every week in Jackie, too!

Love,

The Ed.

Printed and published by D. C. Thomson & Co., Ltd., 185 Fleet Street, London EC4A 2HS. © D. C. Thomson & Co., Ltd., 1983.
ISBN 0 85116 293 2

Maybe we'd never get on "Top of the Pops," but our school's disco dance team was really quite good . . .

With Friends Like Lisa...

That routine you worked out is great, Miss Gordon! It could win us the inter-schools competition.

I'm not sure, Debbie. Something's missing. I think we need another girl in the group.

But who? Everyone who wanted to join has already been given their chance.

Don't worry. We've got time before the competition. Someone might turn up. Now go and get changed or you'll all be late for class.

But just as we were going out . . .

Hey, Peggy, who's that over there?

Oh, that's the new girl, Lisa. She's no-one special.

But there was someone who was special. Very special . . .

And we're dancing our new routine at the school disco next week, Dave. Isn't that great?

Terrific! I'm going steady with a superstar!

Continued on page 8

5

IF YOU'RE ARIES
(Mar. 21-Apr. 20)

How to get noticed

Arians should stick to simple, casual, unfussy clothes.

Your lucky colour's red, so if you can get away with it (and most Arians can) wear bright, dazzling red to go with your bright, dazzling personality and you certainly won't be overlooked!

Which boy to go for

Make straight for the most interesting, exciting boy around. The shy, quiet types just aren't for you.

You'd have a fantastic evening with an Arian or Leo boy, but the relationship might not last long once the party's over. The Arian boy's bossy and so are you, and the Leo boy has a roving eye and likes to play the field.

How to go about getting him

Listening is not your strong point, but if you want to get anywhere with an Aries or Leo boy, give him a chance to do some talking.

With a Leo boy, flattery will work wonders. Just tell him how great you think his clothes/hair/company is, and he'll be yours for the taking.

Best chat-up lines

For the Arian boy — *"Tell me all about yourself."*
For the Leo boy — *"You think you're wonderful, I think you're wonderful, so we agree on something."*

IF YOU'RE TAURUS
(Apr. 21-May 20)

How to get noticed

If you want to shine at your next party, you may have to make a bit of an effort. Strange faces and places tend to make a Taurean feel insecure.

To make the most of yourself, wear an outfit you feel comfortable and at ease in.

Which boy to go for

Your ideal boy is the strong, silent type you can lean on and look up to. A Virgo boy could fit the bill exactly.

You could also strike it lucky with a Capricorn boy, although you might mistake his natural reserve and shyness for lack of interest.

How to go about getting him

Virgos are cautious when it comes to showing their feelings, so don't come on too strong when you first meet your Virgo boy or you could frighten him away. You could also frighten him off if you look in any way outrageous or, horrors, untidy.

Capricorn boys won't care what you look like so long as you're warm, affectionate and above all, sincere.

Best chat-up lines

For the Virgo boy — *"Your shirt looks so clean. What washing powder do you use?"*
For the Capricorn boy — *"You look as lost as I feel. Mind if I join you?"*

IF YOU'RE GEMINI
(May 21-June 20)

How to get noticed

Geminis are bright, sparkling, chatty and cheerful and generally have no problem getting themselves noticed.

To make the most of your personality, go for the feminine approach in your clothes and make-up and be as daring and different as you like. You'll get away with it!

Which boy to go for

A Libra boy is your perfect star mate. To catch his eye you'll have to openly flirt with him, but that should present no problems to someone as practised in the art as a Gemini girl!

If you want an exciting relationship which could cause a few sparks to fly, head for the Gemini boy.

How to go about getting him

The biggest mistake to make with both Libra and Gemini boys is to be too serious too soon. If you want them to notice you, be witty, flirty and unavailable. Don't hang around them all evening waiting for them to make the first move.

Best chat-up lines

For the Libra boy — *"I'd love to dance with you. Can you come back in half-an-hour?"*
For the Gemini boy — *"Haven't I seen you somewhere before? No, I can't have done. Surely I would have remembered you."*

IF YOU'RE CANCER
(June 21-July 21)

How to get noticed

Most Cancer subjects can be a bit moody at times and if this sounds like you, resolve that a party is a place where you leave all your moods behind and concentrate on having a good time. You should go for clothes in romantic, pastel shades rather than dramatic or bright outfits.

Which boy to go for

You'll get on best with a kind, affectionate Taurean boy. He may not be the most exciting of the star signs, but he's reliable and open-hearted.

How to go about getting him

Taurean boys love being mothered and looked after. They also like to eat, so if you want to catch a Taurean boy, all you have to do is walk up to him with a huge bowl of peanuts and start feeding him.

At first, a Taurean boy may seem a bit quiet and cool, but don't mistake that for lack of interest.

Best chat-up lines

For a Taurean boy — *"Would you like me to fetch you a triple decker hamburger with chips?"*

IF YOU'RE LEO
(July 22-Aug. 21)

How to get noticed

Leos are the natural party-goers of the zodiac and you're in your element when you can socialise and mix with lots of different people. You don't need us to tell you to dress up in your most attractive clothes and go to that party feeling, and looking, stunning.

Which boy to go for

Go straight for the tall, good-looking boy who's standing slightly apart from the rest with a slightly haughty, aloof air about him. Chances are he's another Leo and the ideal partner for you.

The other star sign which can hold a lot of attraction for you is fiery and exciting Aries.

How to go about getting him

To catch a Leo boy, all you have to do is use a bit of flattery and then keep on telling him he...

Does the thought of parties fill you with fear? Do you dread yet another evening standing alone in a corner while all around you people seem to be having the time of their lives? If so, now's the time to look to your stars for help. Follow our special astro guide to parties and find out how to get noticed and how to chat up that boy you like, all according to your (and his) star sign.

...nderful he is.

...ou should have no trouble getting an Aries ...y's interest, but if you want to keep him ...erested, you'll have to curb your natural ...o desire to be the centre of attraction.

...est chat-up lines
...or a Leo boy — *"You're fantastic. ...most as fantastic as me, in fact."*
...or an Aries boy — *"I was just telling ...veryone what an interesting person you ...re."*

IF YOU'RE VIRGO
(Aug. 22-Sept. 21)
How to get noticed
You love neat, stylish clothes, so wear a classic dress or smartly co-ordinated outfit to make the most of your personality. Your lucky day is a Friday, so make this the day of the week when you go all out to enjoy yourself.

Which boy to go for
Honest, sincere Capricorn is the ideal boy for you. You won't find him raving about on the dance floor, though. He'll more than likely be the one looking through the records for something less noisy or conducting a deep discussion on the state of the economy.

How to go about getting him
A Capricorn boy enjoys conversation but he likes to laugh, too, and if you can succeed in making him enjoy himself, he'll take notice. He'll also be impressed if you seem to know most of the people at the party. There's a bit of a snob lurking inside every Capricorn.

Best chat-up line
For a Capricorn boy — *"Have you met Princess Diana's cousin? He's an old friend of mine."*

IF YOU'RE LIBRA
(Sept. 22-Oct. 22)
How to get noticed
Librans are very good at giving parties as well as going to them.
Your lucky colours are pink and pale blue and any outfit in those colours will make the most of your natural romantic personality.

Which boy to go for
Look no further than an Aquarius or Sagittarian boy. You'll recognise the Aquarian boy easily. He'll be the one telling people how to Save the Whale or Ban the Bomb.
The Sagittarian boy will be the one surrounded by other girls, so if you want him, you may have to join the queue.

How to go about getting him
You'll certainly gain the attention of the Aquarian boy if you surprise him with a few well-chosen words and startle him by agreeing with him when he's being really outrageous.
You'll have to be active to keep up with the Sagittarian boy's energy and enthusiasm. If you want to be noticed, don't join the admiring throng around him. Do something different. Start a party game in another room; dance by yourself; walk straight up to *him* and ask him to dance — anything to make you stand out from the crowd.

Best chat-up lines
For an Aquarian boy — *"I've just got back from a two-month trip down the Amazon. It was all very boring."*
For a Sagittarian boy — *"I've got five minutes to spare, and I've decided to spend them with you."*

IF YOU'RE SCORPIO
(Oct. 23-Nov. 21)
How to get noticed
It's usually difficult *not* to notice Scorpios. Demanding, emotional and jealous, Scorpios are the most dramatic of all the star signs.
Your choice of party outfit should be dramatic and startling and should ideally have some of your lucky colour, red, in it.

Which boy to go for
If you want a romantic, emotional experience which is anything but dull make straight for an Aries boy. An Aries boy is strong willed, independent and bossy — just the type to tame you.

How to go about getting him
The one thing you shouldn't do with an Arian boy is play games. He has a direct, straightforward approach to life and he expects other people to be the same.

Best chat-up line
For an Aries boy — *"Anything you say is fine by me."*

IF YOU'RE SAGITTARIUS
(Nov. 22-Dec. 21)
How to get noticed
You're the rebel of the zodiac, high spirited, sociable and very independent.
Bright, lively colours suit your personality and you should aim for the casual rather than sophisticated look.

Which boy to go for
Although you're basically uncomplicated and out-going, when it comes to love you're a bit of a dreamer and a romantic Pisces boy is just the one to share your dreams.
If you're looking for a casual, not too serious relationship, though, go for the Aries boy.

How to go about getting him
Don't come on too strong with a Pisces boy or you'll end up frightening him off. He's sensitive and a bit touchy.
A different approach is called for with the Aries boy. If you're too quiet and shy with him, he'll just think you're wet.

Best chat-up lines
For a Pisces boy — *"Don't you think that sometimes words are unnecessary between two people?"*
For an Aries boy — *"No, let me take you home."*

IF YOU'RE CAPRICORN
(Dec. 22-Jan. 19)
How to get noticed
Going to parties doesn't really appeal to your cautious nature unless you know well in advance exactly who's going to be there.
You should take your time getting ready for a party and plan your clothes, hair and make-up well in advance.

Which boy to go for
Few boys are better for the Capricorn girl than a Taurus boy. He's serious, responsible and down-to-earth.
You're also the kind of a girl a Virgo boy will go for. He won't be very romantic, possibly, but he does share your cautious, practical approach to love.

How to go about getting him
Whatever you do, don't rush a Taurus boy into anything. He likes to take things at his own pace, and that includes relationships.
The same cautious approach is called for with

a Virgo boy. Just make sure it isn't *too* cautious, or you could both end up with nothing happening for you at all.

Best chat-up lines
For a Taurus boy — *"That's a nice record. Not for dancing to, of course, just for standing here listening to."*
For a Virgo boy — *"This may sound corny, but do you come here often?"*

IF YOU'RE AQUARIUS
(Jan. 20-Feb. 18)
How to get noticed
You're the dreamer of the zodiac, always a bit apart from the crowd.
Your lucky colour's green, so wear something feminine and floaty in any shade of cool, dreamy green. You like to make an entrance wherever you go, so make sure you arrive a little late and you'll be assured of maximum attention!

Which boy to go for
If you're looking for adventure and excitement, you couldn't do better than a Sagittarian boy.
A like-minded Aquarian boy, though, is probably your ideal partner. Whereas most boys may find you puzzling, he'll understand you perfectly.

How to go about getting him
A Sagittarian boy will want to do all the chasing, so let him. Underneath all his confidence, though, he's a tiny bit anxious about the impression he's making.
When two Aquarians meet, though, there's no need for words. You'll gaze at each other across a crowded room and know that you're destined for one another.

Best chat-up lines
For a Sagittarian boy — *"I'd hate to be a boy and have to make the first move. I could never do it as well as you do."*
For an Aquarian boy — *"I always knew we were meant for each other."*

IF YOU'RE PISCES
(Feb. 19-Mar. 20)
How to get noticed
You're the most feminine of all the star signs and your romantic charm lies in playing the helpless female.
To make the most of your personality, go all out for the completely feminine look in your lucky colours of turquoise or pink.

Which boy to go for
A Cancer boy is just the boy you need to shelter and protect you. Beneath his hard, aggressive shell is a romantic, emotional nature just like your own.
Surprisingly, another good match for you is a Scorpio boy. He'll love you for the way you'll be completely devoted to him.

How to go about getting him
Cancer boys love to be looked after, so fuss over him as much as you like. He'll love you for it!
All you have to do with a Scorpio boy is let him know that he's the only boy in the world as far as you're concerned.

Best chat-up lines
For a Cancer boy — *"You mean you actually know how a motor bike engine works? You must be ever so clever."*
For a Scorpio boy — *"There's no-one else in the whole world I'd rather be with than you."*

Continued from page 5

But Miss Gordon's right. We do need another girl. Is there anyone good enough and keen enough, though?

You'll find someone, love. Now I've got to dash. I'll see you later, OK?

OK, Dave. Bye.

THERE'S THAT NEW GIRL AGAIN. SHE LOOKS A BIT LOST. POOR THING, IT MUST BE AWFUL STARTING AT A NEW SCHOOL IN THE MIDDLE OF TERM.

Hi. You're Lisa, aren't you? I'm Debbie. I'm in your year, so if you've got any problems with anything, just ask.

Em . . . yes, OK. Th-thanks, Debbie. It's not easy being a new girl. Everyone's got their own friends and boyfriends. They don't need me.

Don't be silly. Of course they do! For a start, if you're any good at dancing, the disco team needs you! We'll be auditioning for another girl soon. Why not give it a try?

Me! In the dance team? I'd like to, but I—I don't know if I could . . .

Of course you could! It's easy! Just come to the audition and see what happens. It would be one way to make friends, anyway, wouldn't it?

Yes, I suppose it would. Thanks, Debbie. I—I don't know why you're being so nice to me, though.

Purely selfish motives! We need a new girl in the dance team! Oh—and remember—the school disco is next week. You'll have the chance to meet lots of people there.

I have to admit, though, I didn't give Lisa another thought after that. Until on the day of the disco . . .

Lisa, you're crying! What's wrong?

I-I'm just being silly. I've n-nothing nice to wear tonight and no-one to go with. And I was looking forward to it so much, too.

Hey, cheer up. I can lend you a dress. And I'll help you get ready, if you like. Then you can come along with me and my boyfriend, Dave. How does that sound?

Oh, Debbie, it—it sounds wonderful. I don't know how to thank you.

She'd certainly cheered up by that evening. In fact, in my dress and with make-up on, she looked like a different person.

That's the third guy who's asked you to dance, Lisa. Didn't you like any of them?

Oh, Debbie, yes, of course I did. But I-I'm not used to boys wanting to dance with me. It makes me nervous and I wouldn't know what to say to them. Silly, isn't it?

No, it's not silly, Lisa. And you won't be shy with Dave, I hope. I've got to change now for our dance routine, so he'll look after you. He might even convince you that boys are quite nice, really!

Oh, I don't feel shy with Dave.

Debbie's so lucky, being in the dance team and having a super boyfriend like you, Dave. How does she do it?

I don't know about her being lucky, Lisa. I reckon I'm the lucky one.

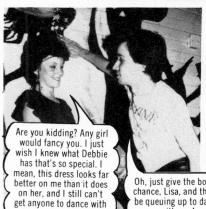

Are you kidding? Any girl would fancy you. I just wish I knew what Debbie has that's so special. I mean, this dress looks far better on me than it does on her, and I still can't get anyone to dance with me.

Oh, just give the boys a chance, Lisa, and they'll be queuing up to dance with you!

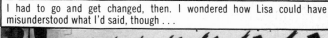

And later, when we'd finished our number . . .

You were great! All of you!

I agree with Miss Gordon now, though. We do need another girl.

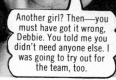

Another girl? Then—you must have got it wrong, Debbie. You told me you didn't need anyone else. I was going to try out for the team, too.

I couldn't believe my ears!

Why on earth did you say that, Deb? You know we need another girl!

But I-I didn't say that. Of course Lisa can try out for the team if she wants to. I'm sorry if she got the wrong impression.

I had to go and get changed, then. I wondered how Lisa could have misunderstood what I'd said, though . . .

Don't worry about Dave, Debbie! I'll look after him till you come back.

Yes, OK, Lisa.

IT'S SILLY, BUT SOMEHOW I DON'T LIKE LEAVING THEM ALONE TOGETHER. THERE'S SOMETHING ABOUT LISA. SOMETHING I DON'T QUITE TRUST . . .

As the days went on, there were other things, too . . .

That was a bit selfish of you, Debbie. You might at least have left Lisa with enough to get home.

Don't worry about that £1 you borrowed from me, Debbie. It was my last one, but Peggy says she'll lend me the money for my bus fare.

But—I didn't borrow anything. I don't know what she's talking about.

She kept bothering Dave too.

Dave, I really need help with my Maths homework. Could you spare me an hour after school? Debbie says you don't like to help people, but I don't believe that.

Of course I'll help you, Lisa. I don't understand why Debbie said I wouldn't.

I DIDN'T SAY IT, DAVE. BUT IT WON'T DO ME ANY GOOD TO DENY IT. I'M BEGINNING TO SEE HOW LISA OPERATES . . .

Continued on page 12

Brilliant Brush Strokes

1. Eyelash brush

2. Eyeliner brush

3. Complexion brush

4. Sponge applicators

5. Wedge-shaped eye-shadow brush

6. Lip brush

IF you want a professional finish to your make-up, invest in a few brushes! You can buy them individually or in kits, and once you learn how to use them, you'll be able to blend make-up colours better and achieve cleaner lines, too.

Eyelash Brush

These are handy even if you normally use a wand mascara, as you can brush a little oil on to your lashes to condition them on the days you go mascaraless. Normally, they're used to apply cake or block mascara which is dampened with water before using the brush to take up the colour. Apply several coats, leaving time in between for the mascara to dry — first apply to top side of upper lashes, stroking the colour down, then apply to the underside of the top lashes, stroking the colour up, and lastly apply to the lower lashes.

Complexion Brush

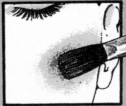

Use this fairly thick brush to dust off surplus face powder and then to apply powder blusher on top of both foundation and powder. Begin the blusher under the middle of your eye and brush it outwards along your cheekbone towards the hairline. Avoid positioning it too close to your nose or eye. You could keep a spare complexion brush to brush away any traces of powder eye shadow that fall on to your cheeks while you're doing your eyes, too.

Wedge-Shaped Eye-Shadow Brush

This is useful for applying shadow to the socket area. It's also useful for applying a little shadow under the bottom lashes for making extended wing shapes at the corners of the eyes.

Eyeliner Brush

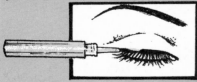

Although liquid liners usually come with brushes it's helpful to have a separate brush as it means you can turn eyeshadows into liners by either dipping the brush into cream shadows, or wetting, then dipping your brush into powder shadows. Applying eyeliner needs a good brush and a steady hand or it will look messy, so get some practice in before any important event!

Sponge Applicator

These are so cheap you can afford several. Keep at least a long-handled and a short-handled one to allow you freedom of movement when applying eye-shadow over your entire eyelid. Since they're sponge they're easy to keep clean — just wash in a little soapy water, so preventing any irritation to the eye.

Lip brush

A lip brush will not only give a better shape to your lips but it also means you can get down to the very last drop of your lipstick! Powder round the edges of your mouth first to avoid lip colour running, then draw the lip shape you want with the brush, then fill it in. Use your brush to apply lip gloss on top, too.

KNIT WITS!

Clever little extras to knit up in a night!

Knit yourself these matching accessories with a difference and look good and keep warm at the same time! Designed by Alan Dart, these unusual fingerless mittens and ankle warmers take just two balls of wool and are so easy, even the Ed only took one evening to knit them up!

LEGWARMERS AND MITTENS

YARN — Two x 100 g balls of Sirdar Gemini Brushed Chunky.

NEEDLES — A pair each of 5½ mm and 6½ mm, and a stitch holder.

TENSION — 13½ sts and 19 rows to 10 cm square, measured over stocking-stitch on 6½ mm needles.

ABBREVIATIONS — K — knit, P — purl, st(s) — stitch(es), cont — continue, comm — commencing, st-st — stocking-stitch, one row knit, one row purl, inc — increase, beg — beginning.

LEGWARMERS

With 5½ mm needles cast on 32 sts and work 14 rows K1, P1 rib.
Change to 6½ mm needles and cont in st-st comm with a K row.

Work 5 rows.
Inc (by working into front and back of st) 1 st at beg and end of next and every following 5th row until there are 46 sts on the needle.
Cont without shaping for 10 rows, ending with a P row.
Change to 5½ mm needles and work 8 rows K1, P1 rib.
Cast off in rib.

MITTENS

With 5½ mm needles cast on 26 sts and work 10 rows K1, P1 rib.
Change to 6½ mm needles and cont in st-st comm with a K row.
Row 1 — K.
Row 2 and all alternate rows — P.
Row 3 — K13, inc (by working into horizontal thread before next st), K13.
Row 5 — K13, inc, K1, inc, K13.
Row 7 — K13, inc, K3, inc, K13.

Row 9 — K13, inc, K5, inc, K13.
Row 11 — K13, inc, K7, inc, K13.
Row 12 — P.
Next row — K13, slip these sts on to a stitch holder, with 5½ mm needles work 9 sts in K1, P1 rib, slip remaining 13 sts on to a stitch holder.
Work 3 rows P1, K1 rib on these 9 sts.
Cast off loosely in rib.
Slip the first set of held sts on to a 6½ mm needle, rejoin yarn to the remaining held sts, and with 6½ mm needles K to end (26 sts).
Next row — P.
Change to 5½ mm needles and work 4 rows K1, P1 rib.
Cast off loosely in rib.

TO MAKE UP

Do not press work. Join seams on legwarmers. Darn in yarn at base of thumbs. Join thumb seams. Join seams of mittens.

Continued from page 9

She even came between Dave and me when we were alone together.

I'm sorry I'm late, Debbie. Lisa needed some more help with that Maths homework.

Yes, I'm sure she did. I'm beginning to think she's not quite so dumb at Maths as she makes out.

That's not a very nice thing to say. Lisa's trying really hard to be friendly and I think you ought to give her a chance. She's very nice once you get to know her.

Oh yes? And just how well have you got to know her?

I'll pretend I didn't hear that remark. Honestly, Debbie, ever since Lisa's appeared on the scene, you've changed. She's really upset by your attitude. She thinks you're jealous of her.

Dave—can't you see what she's doing? She doesn't like me. She tells lies about me. She's turning everyone against me— even you!

I couldn't help it. I just burst into tears.

Don't cry, love. You're just a bit nervous about the dance competition, probably. And you mustn't mind about Lisa. Just try being a bit nicer to her, that's all.

Yes, alright, Dave. I'll try

MAYBE HE'S RIGHT. MAYBE I AM IMAGINING THINGS. SHE'S AUDITIONING FOR THE TEAM TOMORROW. WE'LL SEE WHAT HAPPENS THEN.

But at the audition, I realised once and for all that it wasn't just my imagination . . .

That's very good, Lisa! Good enough for the team in fact! Now Debbie, keep concentrating!

LISA'S COMING REALLY CLOSE TO ME. SHE'LL TRIP ME UP IF SHE'S NOT CAREFUL.

But she was too clever for that .

She kicked me! Debbie, how could you! I could have twisted my ankle or anything! Then I wouldn't have had a chance to be in the team.

Debbie! I'm shocked at such dreadful behaviour! Apologise to Lisa at once!

I'm sorry if I kicked you, Lisa.

I WOULD BE SORRY IF I HAD. BUT I DIDN'T. YOU ENGINEERED THAT LITTLE FALL.

That's all right, Debbie. And I don't believe you did it on purpose, no matter what it looked like.

She got her place on the team, of course, and the sympathy of everyone.

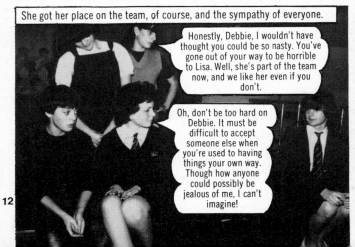

Honestly, Debbie, I wouldn't have thought you could be so nasty. You've gone out of your way to be horrible to Lisa. Well, she's part of the team now, and we like her even if you don't.

Oh, don't be too hard on Debbie. It must be difficult to accept someone else when you're used to having things your own way. Though how anyone could possibly be jealous of me, I can't imagine!

Lisa, we're off for a coffee now. Are you coming?

In a minute. I just want to speak to Debbie.

Honestly, Lisa, I don't know how you can be so nice to her after the way she's treated you.

I'm sure you're wrong about her, Peggy. Just let me have a word with her and I'll catch you up later.

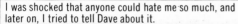

And once they'd gone . . .

Well, Lisa, you've turned my friends against me and you've messed things up between Dave and me. But why? What have I ever done to you except try to be friendly?

You always pretend to like me—at first. But you don't really. It's just a big act.

Well, now it's my turn. I'm going to take Dave, your friends, and your place on the dance team! Then you'll be the outsider!

I was shocked that anyone could hate me so much, and later on, I tried to tell Dave about it.

. . .and that's exactly what she said to me! I felt a bit sorry for her, actually.

Debbie, I'm warning you, everyone's talking about how nasty you are to Lisa. If I were you, I wouldn't repeat that crazy story to anyone else. And I don't want to hear it again, either!

OH DAVE, PLEASE DON'T LET HER SPOIL THINGS BETWEEN US. PLEASE . . .

For the next few days I kept out of her way as much as possible. It was difficult at rehearsals for the dance competition, though.

Now girls, this is the last dress rehearsal. As you know, Debbie will be leader and main dancer and Lisa will be her stand-in.

LISA WANTED THE LEAD, I KNOW. BUT THE COMPETITION'S TOMORROW NIGHT, SO THERE'S NOTHING SHE CAN DO ABOUT THIS. NOTHING.

But I was wrong. So wrong . . .

Well girls, this is it. The inter-schools competition. You'll do well, I know. Now all I need is a volunteer to collect the costumes. They're all cleaned and pressed and hanging up in the Form Room.

I'll get them, Miss Gordon. It'll give Debbie a chance to calm down. I think she's a bit nervous.

I'M NOT GOING TO LET HER UPSET ME. THAT'S EXACTLY WHAT SHE WANTS TO HAPPEN, THEN SHE'LL TAKE MY PLACE. BUT SHE'S NOT GOING TO GET THE CHANCE.

But I wouldn't have felt so confident if I'd seen what was happening in the Form Room . . .

TEARING THE COSTUME WILL MAKE SURE I GET TO DANCE THE LEAD. AND IT'LL MAKE SURE DEBBIE DOESN'T GET TO DANCE AT ALL!

The next thing I knew . . .

I didn't know you hated me this much, Debbie. It's bad enough sneaking in early and tearing my costume to stop me from going on, but didn't you think about the team? They'll be one short now. Well, I hope you're satisfied.

B-but I didn't . . .

I'll just have to drop out now. The only other costume that fits me is Debbie's—and she'll be wearing hers.

Yes, Miss Gordon. That's only fair. We wouldn't want to dance with Debbie now, anyway.

No, Lisa. In the circumstances, I think Debbie should drop out and let you take her place. In fact, I insist on it.

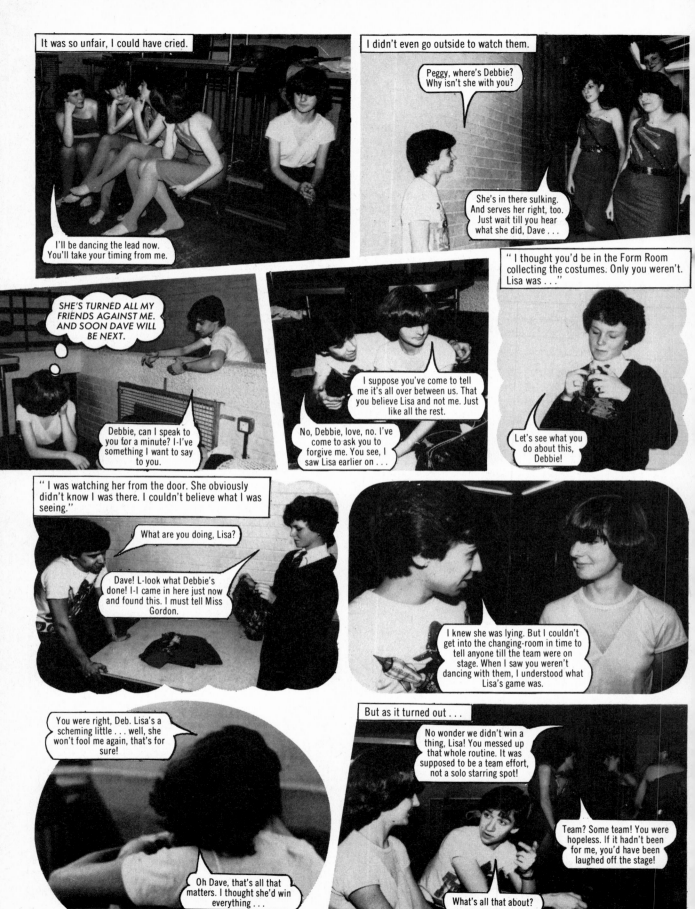

14

Continued on page 16

Don't let the Christmas Creeps creep up on YOU!

Christmas is coming—and with it come the Christmas Creeps. Christmas does funny things to some boys and OK, so it is a time for love, but there is a limit. So if you don't want to get crept up on by a Christmas Creep this year, read on and find out how to recognise them—and how to get rid of them!

THE CREEPY COUSIN

Your mum's just announced that she's invited your aunt for Christmas lunch. This means that your cousin, who's slimier than green gunge but who thinks he's as irresistible as chocolate meringue, will be there as well. He'll sit there, leering across at you, chewing and slavering over a turkey leg, making it obvious he wishes it was you he was chewing and slavering over.

Then he offers to help you with the washing-up and you find yourself alone in the kitchen with him. He makes remarks like, "I loved your mum's Christmas pudding, but you're the sweet I'd really like to get my teeth into" and, "It may be cold outside but you're hot enough for me." Then he sidles along the sink towards you and you know you're in for the greatest battle since King Kong met the Thing from the Swamp. You know that once he makes a grab for you, he'll never let go, so . . .

. . . hand him a trifle dish and let it slip before he takes it. Then scream, "Mum! He's broken your best crystal!"

. . . say to him, "Your mum was telling me you never go anywhere without your blue, fluffy teddy. She says you call him Boofles. I think that's really sweet."

. . . slap him about the face with a wet dishcloth saying, "You shouldn't have eaten that turkey leg. Now you've got grease all over your face and hair. Or is it natural?"

THE STEAMY SANTA

You've taken your little brother / sister / niece / nephew to see Santa in his grotto at the local department store. Santa's a cheerful-looking, chubby figure sitting at the far end, all jolly and festive—until he sees you. Then you suddenly notice he's paying more attention to you than to your little brother / sister / niece / nephew and there's more than a Merry Christmas twinkle in his eye. He fancies you! Santa!!

You stand there, trying not to notice him leering at you under his beard, then he pats his over-friendly knee, winks at you and mutters darkly, "Come and sit on my knee little girl and tell me what you'd like for Christmas . . ." There's no way you want to encourage the old fool and you certainly don't want to sit on his knee, so . . .

. . . say, "How nice. But I can tell just by looking at you that you're a very tired old man and I wouldn't like to make your rheumatism any worse."

. . . say, in as loud a voice as possible, "What I want for Christmas is a bit of respect, and that's clearly something I'm not going to get from you."

. . . laugh lightly and say, "Oh, wait till I tell Daddy. He'll be so pleased to hear he's employed a Santa who's so friendly to his customers."

THE MISTLETOE MAULER

Every office party, school dance or college disco has at least one of these. You'll have noticed him around at work / school / college and thought he looked a total turn-off in his shiny suit, his nylon shirt with his vest showing through and his pockets bulging with old chip papers, acne pills, dust and dandruff. Normally he never bothers anyone—until the Christmas party / dance / disco arrives—and with it, the Magic Mistletoe.

The Mistletoe Mauler thinks that a piece of mistletoe has magical properties which transform him into every girl's dream (instead of every girl's nightmare). So there you are, all decked out in tinsel and glitter, eyeing up some dishy boy who'll do nicely, when the mauler decides to make his move. He advances on you, greasy hair and acne shining in the festive lighting, half a Twiglet sticking to his cheek, holding the magic mistletoe aloft. Now, you know you're going to be ill if he kisses you, so . . .

. . . sneeze right in his face and tell him they're admitting you to a sanitorium after Christmas to cure your highly contagious chest infection.

. . . burst out laughing, give him a push, and say, "I didn't know I was on Game For A Laugh!"

. . . turn your head away quickly, saying, "I've just seen my friend come in." You'll get a slobbery, deafening, unpleasant sensation as he makes contact with your left ear, but think what you'd have got otherwise.

THE PLODDING POSTMAN

If you live in a biggish town, it's quite likely that the Post Office will be employing some students to deliver the Christmas post. Oh Goodie, you think, all those dishy young postmen waiting to be invited in for a cup of tea and a nice warm cuddle.

But, horrors, out of all the dishy postmen about, you have to get the wet, weedy one. He wears his college scarf with pride and plods around the neighbourhood with his red nose, complete with drip on the end, stuck in an Algebra book. His face brightens on approaching your house and he obviously wants to spend all day standing on your doorstep talking about his mum, his ambition to become an accounts clerk, his Aunt Maud who's knitting him a vest and socks for Christmas, and his plans for the evening — which include you. So . . .

. . . answer the door in rollers, no make-up, and have a plate of burnt mince pies in your hand. Say, "This is the real me. When can I meet your mum?"

. . . leave a note on the door saying, "Christmas 'male' has been cancelled due to total lack of interest. Please leave next door."

. . . make a tape-recording of an enormous wolfhound growling and snarling and play it as he plods up the path. If you actually own a growling, snarling wolfhound, you won't have a problem with plodding postmen. Or any other postmen, come to that.

Continued from page 14

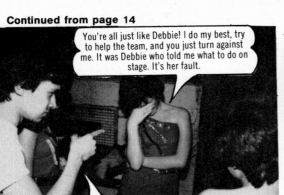

You're all just like Debbie! I do my best, try to help the team, and you just turn against me. It was Debbie who told me what to do on stage. It's her fault.

That's enough, Lisa! I don't want to listen to any more of your lies.

Dave told the girls what he'd seen . . .

She's been deliberately turning us against Debbie. I'm sorry to say I nearly fell for it.

B-but Dave, I . . . I only . . .

Next moment, she just collapsed into tears.

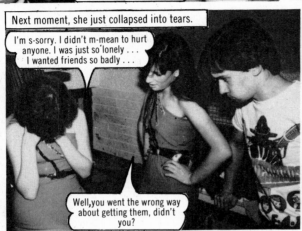

I'm s-sorry. I didn't m-mean to hurt anyone. I was just so lonely . . . I wanted friends so badly . . .

Well, you went the wrong way about getting them, didn't you?

No, don't shout at her any more. I think she seems to have paid for what she did.

I'm sorry, Debbie, so sorry for the trouble I caused. C-can you ever forgive me . . ?

It won't be easy, Lisa. But maybe we can forgive and forget. That's the best way to make friends.

Th-thanks, Debbie. I . . . I don't know why you should be so nice to me.

Well, I suppose now I know what it's like to feel lonely, and cut off from everyone. It's not a very nice feeling.

No, it's not. I should know. And thank you. Thank you all. I'll never cause any more trouble again.

No, I don't believe you will, Lisa.

But perhaps if I'd seen what happened later, I wouldn't have been so sure . . .

OH, THERE'S PEGGY'S BOYFRIEND WAITING FOR HER. MMMM . . . HE'S QUITE NICE . . .

Hi, Steve. Peggy wants me to take you for a coffee. She says she'll be along later.

Oh. She didn't say anything to me about it. But if you say so, I suppose it's all right.

With friends like Lisa, this is not—**THE END**

Resolutionary Ideas !

Our New Year resolution is to help these pop stars with theirs. Mind you, they'll probably resolve to get us back for this!

Andy McClusky, O.M.D.
"I resolve faithfully to give up my part-time job and concentrate fully on my music career. After all, being a Morse code messenger for the Navy is really lowering my standards! (Geddit?!) I also promise to try to smile at least once this year!"

Musical Youth
"We resolve to stop getting so bored at photo sessions! I mean, if we've not got some comics, Frisbees and streamers — we just can't go through with it!
"Kelvin's also resolved to stop singing 'Be-diddley-diddley, dum' in a deep voice on *all* our records!"

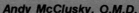

Marc Almond, Soft Cell
"I resolve to wash my dishes more than once a week. I honestly try to do them every day, but those soap suds play havoc with my bangles!"

Phil Oakey, Human League
"I resolve to cut down on all those nasty sweets and choccy biccies I've been scoffing recently 'cos I'm fed up with everyone calling me Chubby-Chops!
"I also, cough, choke, splutter, resolve to stop having my pic taken in smoky studios. Never mind the sultry atmosphere, my eyes are stinging!"

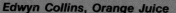

Edwyn Collins, Orange Juice
"I resolve to stop dressing up in silly clothes like my Boy Scout outfit. I'm getting sick of folk asking me if I'm doing 'Bob-A-Job'!
"Oh, it's no use, I probably won't keep this promise. I'd better 'Rip It Up And Start Again!' Hey, that sounds like a great title for a song!"

THE SHAPE OF

Slip into something comfy, switch on shape-up exercises!

SOME of these exercises may already be familiar to you so you'll be able to do them without even looking at these pages. The order you should do them in follows a pattern that's easy to get the hang of, too; you begin with easy warm up exercises, move on to slightly more strenuous ones, then finish up with some relaxing and refreshing floor movements.

If you haven't exercised for a while, do each exercise slowly so your muscles can get used to working, then, as you become stronger, step up the tempo. Don't ever force yourself to do an exercise if it feels uncomfortable, but do try to do more of each exercise at each successive session or you'll never see the benefits.

Try to do this set at least three times a week, and don't wait more than thirty - six hours between sessions or your muscles will go all stiff again and you'll be back to square one!

Ready? Steady? Go!

Inhale and exhale deeply before you start, then breathe in through your nose and out through your mouth you work out. Remember to hold your tummy in and tighten your buttocks, pushing them slightly forward as you work, and you'll soon see improvements in those two areas!

1 TIPS TO TOE

Stand with your legs apart and bend from the waist without bending your knees. Then swing your left hand down across your body to touch your right foot. Repeat with other arm and foot. Begin with ten swings and build up to fifty.

2 BENDY BENDY

Now slide your left arm down your left side as far as it will go, at the same time swinging your right arm over your head. Stretch as you go so you feel your waist muscles pull. Work up to fifty bends to each side.

8 SCISSOR SNIP

Lie down on your side and prop your head up, leaning on your elbow. Swing your leg up as high as it will go and bring it down again. Repeat ten times. Turn over to lie on your other leg. Do this scissor kick fairly quickly for the best results and build up to doing twenty each side.

18

YOU TO COME!

ome music and stretch and bend your body with some simple

3 BOUNCE FOR BOUNCE

Bend your whole body forward from the waist and bounce down then relax and bounce again until you can grab both ankles with your hands. You should feel the muscles at the back of your thighs stretch as you do this one.

Once you can grab your ankles, hold for a count of ten and relax, after letting go! *Tired? Those were just your warm ups – now on to the strenuous section!*

6 WING AWAY

This should improve your posture. Stand as straight as you can, arms outstretched, and slowly raise and lower your body with a series of knee bends. You should feel the muscles in your legs stretch if you're doing this one correctly. Do ten times, build up to twenty-five.

4 LEGS UP

This exercise should shift "jodhpur" thighs and also streamline your waist. Unless you've got a great sense of balance, hold on to a chair with one hand as you do this. Kick your leg out to the side, trying to get it a little higher each time. Grasp your ankle and hold this position for a few minutes until you feel the pull on your muscles. If done properly, it should be difficult to do more than ten of these each side at a time!

5 LEG STRETCHES

This is good for posture, the back, and stretching the muscles on the inside of the thighs. It's based on a yoga exercise so should be done fairly slowly with steady, deep breathing. Sit on the floor and bring your feet together, grasping your ankles.

With a bouncing movement, try to get your knees to touch the floor. At first you'll be really stiff so don't force your legs, work up to this one!

7 WHEELIES

Lie on the floor and relax for a few minutes before pushing your legs up and, supporting your back, begin cycling in the air.

Cycle quite quickly for at least a few minutes or for as long as you can. This is an easy and relaxing exercise since your weight is supported on the large area of your back rather than the much smaller area of your feet.

Who's Your Star Boy?

ARIES

Weak and wishy-washy specimens aren't for you, so keep your eyes peeled for a guy with a strong personality — and a touch of bossiness, too! Your ideal guy's the original soft-centre — a toughie with a heart of gold — whose unpredictable moods keep your interest. It's just as well, really, as any other boy would bore you to tears!

TAURUS

*Your star boy must be the steady, reliable type to keep you — a fiery, jealous Taurean - on the rails. Strictly no super-bores, though! You're an avid fan of the beautiful things in life, and as far as you're concerned, looks **are** pretty important. The traditional good-looker's the one for you — someone you'll love to show off — and if he has a wealthy Dad, so much the better!*

GEMINI

Your main problem's boredom, so you'll hanker for a fella full of tricks and surprises — a real joker, in fact! You dream of being swept off your feet in a whirlwind romance, and your star boy's one who'll shower you with pressies, never taking you for granted. He's pretty intelligent, too, as he knows that keeping you entertained is the only way he'll stop your heart from wandering!

Your birth sign plays a pretty important part in your life, and it affects your relationships, too! If you're not sure which type of guy you'd be happiest with, read on — he's the one for you!

CANCER

You need the security of a serious, emotional relationship, so it stands to reason that your ideal boy's the deep and sensitive type, too! He'll play the part of protecting little you, and he'll understand that you've a need to be pampered, so he'll give way to your whims. And as you're a true romantic, you'll feel that once you've met him, you're sure to live happily ever after . . .

LEO

You're affectionate, fun to be with and a real chatterbox — only if you're with someone you're genuinely fond of, though! Choose your guy carefully — he'll be the pick of the bunch, the boy the others follow — with more than his fair share of confidence. Being a strong-minded, ambitious Leo, you'll expect your fella to want to get on in the world, too!

VIRGO

A run-of-the-mill boy isn't for you – no, you're on the lookout for someone extra-special! Your ideal guy's sensitive and thoughtful, taking you as seriously as you do him, and living up to your high expectations. He's pretty tolerant, too, as you're not the easiest among us to get along with at times! You won't find him at the disco or on the football pitch, but he's well worth looking out for!

LIBRA

Love plays an essential part in your life, so your star boy's extra important to you! He's sociable and fun, keeping the conversation bubbling along — which is just as well, really, as nothing turns you off more than an over-serious, jealous type. When you're with your boy, you steer clear of squabbles, and with your ideal boy, it's fun and laughs all the way!

SCORPIO

A casual relationship won't hold your interest for long, so the guy for you is an intense type – and pretty possessive with it! You thrive on storms and squabbles, enjoying the excitement of falling out and making up yet again, so it's essential that your star boy has more than an average helping of patience.

SAGITTARIUS

Wet blankets? You'll put up with no such things, and your ideal fella will be expected to be sparkling and fun twenty-four hours a day! For you, love and friendship go together, and rather than just someone to go out with, you're looking for a very special someone who's great company when you need them.

CAPRICORN

*It's vital that your fella's someone you respect and admire, so he must be on your level in every way. No thickies for you – he'll be intelligent and responsible – you won't find **this** guy flying off the handle! – with great ambitions for the future. Yes, this boy certainly knows where he's going and how to get there!*

AQUARIUS

Your mates may find your taste in fellas a little strange — but you purposely keep your eyes peeled for unusual specimens, the guys that stand out from the crowd! Your ideal relationship won't be stifling or constricting. You'll have great times together, and your boy will be brimming over with original ideas. One word of warning, though — Mum'll think he's a right weirdo!

PISCES

Love and romantic daydreams are the very essence of your life, so your star boy's a pretty fantastic person! He's poetic and passionate, ready to fling himself into the romance of the century – and you'll be able to trust him absolutely. Don't be afraid to come down to earth once in a while, though 'cos fellas like these are few and far between!

We all have to go on first dates at some point in our lives and they're not always successful. But why? Read on to find out how to avoid those first-date disasters!

FIRST DATE PITFALLS

YOU'VE got yourself a brand-new boy and you're about to meet him for your first real date. Everything looks lovely. It'll be wonderful. Nothing can possibly go wrong . . .

Except *First-Date Pitfalls*—and that's the end of another promising romance. They're the mistakes that make the first-date girl clutch her brow and moan, ''I shouldn't have done *that*!'' as her new guy hares off up the road in a cloud of dust!

Here are just a few:

I SHOULDN'T HAVE . . . got his name wrong. His name's Bill and he reckons he's made such a good impression on you that you'll remember him for ever. Or even longer. But you turn up for that first date and say, ''Hi, Sid, . . . er, Frank . . . er, Arthur?'' This gives him the impression that he's not quite as memorable as he thought he was and he's likely to go right off you immediately.

But forgetting his name isn't as bad as forgetting what he looks like and walking right past him as he stands at the meeting place with a welcoming smile.

I SHOULDN'T HAVE . . . eaten garlic. Chomping through a garlic-riddled meal before going on that first date isn't a good idea. It'll put him right off the idea of kissing you, and if you've really overdone the garlic flavouring he may even wear a gas mask, which will make conversation difficult. Don't kid yourself that you've had a lucky escape and the garlic has scared him off 'cos he's a vampire. He probably isn't.

I SHOULDN'T HAVE . . . introduced him to my best friend. Not if your best friend is a beautiful man-eater, you shouldn't. It's no fun turning up at the disco to show off your fabulous new boyfriend and then having to walk home on your own, mumbling tearfully, while your dishy best friend waltzes off with him. Keep him to yourself for a while, until you get used to each other. Once he's really got to know you he's not so likely to be snatched. Unless you're incredibly bad-tempered and spotty and horrible. Which you're not, are you? Well, not all three.

I SHOULDN'T HAVE . . . turned up late. Remember the guy doesn't know you all that well. All he knows is that you agreed to a date and you've had a whole night and a day to change your mind. So he's a bit scared of being made a fool of and isn't going to spend too long waiting for a girl who may not turn up at all. If you do turn up late and are lucky enough to find him still standing there like a lemon, have a good excuse. Something to soften him up, like: ''I had to stop to rescue a drowning puppy from the lake.'' Or: ''I was caught in a rainstorm and had to go back home to change.'' If you're very late and he's looking a little tight around the mouth, make it two puppies (or even four), or a freak hurricane.

I SHOULDN'T HAVE . . . taken him home. Dragging the guy home to meet the folks on the first date is a bad idea. The guy has used up most of his available nerve in asking you for a date in the first place. Having to be stared at critically by Mum, Dad, Gran, Aunt Ethel, the budgie and the cat will put him under more strain than the human mind can stand. So don't take him home until he's relaxed enough to cope with it. This could take months, especially if your Aunt Ethel is anything like everybody else's Aunt Ethel.

I SHOULDN'T HAVE . . . arrived for the date in the wrong clothes. It's a good idea to find out roughly what he's got planned for that first date. It won't help much if you turn up in your dolliest dress to find him standing with his greasy motor bike, all dressed up in leathers and ready to bomb off to a grass-track meeting. Or if you arrive in your scruffiest gear expecting to bomb off on his bike while he's immaculate in his best suit and has booked a table for two at the Ritz.

I SHOULDN'T HAVE . . . mentioned my last boyfriend. Keep your last guy out of it. If you say nice things about him, like what a great dancer he was, or how he used to throw his jacket over puddles for you to walk on, your new guy will be worried about how he's going to match up to such a wonderful person. He'll also be wondering how you lost Mr Wonderful. Is there something about you he doesn't know?

And if you try to make the new guy feel good by saying rotten things about your last boy, that won't work either. New guy will have the uneasy feeling that you'll be saying nasty things about him when you move on to your next fella.

I SHOULDN'T HAVE . . . insisted on going to the pictures. He's going to be doing his best to please on that first date, but when he says, ''Where do you fancy going?'' don't pick on something expensive, just in case he's flat broke. It can be embarrassing watching a poor guy blushing hotly as he sorts through a collection of small change, shirt buttons and dead moths, trying to get enough cash together for two seats in the stalls. Offering to go dutch is fine, but paying the whole lot yourself isn't going to make him feel much better. So settle for a walk on that first date and a couple of Cokes in a café. He'll appreciate it and it'll prove you're not the kind of girl who's trying to rip him off. Of course, once you've discovered that he's *incredibly* rich . . . that's different.

So think hard before going on that first date. Avoid the *First-Date Pitfalls* and have a great time. That way you won't crawl miserably home, moaning, ''*I shouldn't have . . .*''

A Jackie Short Story By Jo Reade

Time to Love Again

I'd never be free of Steve, not as long as he filled my thoughts and my heart. There was only one thing to be done – I'd have to say goodbye to him forever.

I WOKE up and blinked at the ceiling, feeling snug and warm and happy. From far off I could hear the bells of St Martin's Church. Christmas morning.

I curled myself into a comfortable ball and dreamily remembered last night's Christmas Eve party — with Peter. It was a lovely party, but being there with Peter made it even better. We'd had a great time. The whole evening seemed now just a blur of dancing, eating, laughing, drinking. But in all the blur, one memory was clear; Peter kissing me under the mistletoe and holding me tight.

"And he's coming to see me today," I said to myself, wiggling my toes. "So he must be keen."

Peter was sort of special. I think I knew it when I first saw him at the disco in late November. Our eyes met and I felt an instant electric tingle running up my spine. He liked me, too. I could tell. I danced with him but I wouldn't let him walk me home, although I wanted to.

I tried hard to resist him too, but we kept meeting accidentally and I kept finding myself looking into his warm blue eyes and thinking dreamy thoughts about him. I just couldn't stop myself liking him. But I hadn't given in until he invited me to the Christmas Eve party.

After that mistletoe kiss, he'd gazed down into my eyes and said, "I've been wanting to do that since I first saw you, Sara. How come it's taken me so long to get to know you? I was beginning to think you didn't like me."

And I'd said, "I like you, Peter. I really do." And we'd kissed again, under the mistletoe.

So there I was, curled up warm in bed on Christmas morning, thinking about Peter and feeling happy. But it didn't last. Because it wasn't fair to Steve.

Steve had been special to me, too, not so long ago. Just the way Peter was now. What we'd had together seemed so good I never thought another boy could come into my life. But it had happened. And I felt guilty and sad about Steve. How could I do this to him? I hadn't wanted it to happen, though. I'd tried to resist my feelings for Peter but, in the end, they'd been too strong.

I got up and washed and dressed. The church bells still rang. Christmas Day was frosty cold but the sky was clear and there was no snow.

I went downstairs. My dad was in the sitting room, piling the parcels around the tree. He kissed me on the cheek and hugged me like a great bear.

"Happy Christmas, Sara," he boomed.

"Happy Christmas, Dad," I replied, but I wasn't feeling happy.

He pointed to the brightly-wrapped parcels. "I bet you can't wait to open yours," he grinned.

It was our family custom to open our Christmas presents after the Christmas meal. Yesterday I'd been impatient to know what was in my parcels. Now it didn't seem to matter. But I pretended I was still excited.

I went into the kitchen. Mum was peeling potatoes. The turkey was already in the oven, and the smell of it roasting was beginning to fill the air.

"Happy Christmas, Sara dear," Mum said.

"Happy Christmas, Mum. Can I help?"

She smiled. "No, I'm well organised — everything's under control. Thanks just the same."

"I think I'll go for a walk, then," I said.

"Good idea. It'll give you an appetite. You'll need it. Dad's bought an even bigger turkey this year. I could hardly get it into the oven."

"If a boy should call before I get back," I began, "tell him . . ."

She looked at me. "A boy?"

"His name's Peter. Tell him I won't be long."

"Peter," she repeated thoughtfully.

Yes, I thought. *Peter. Not Steve. Not any more.*

"I'll tell him," she said. "Sara . . . I'm glad."

I nodded and turned away, not able to look into her eyes any longer.

I went out to the hall and put on my coat.

Yes, Mum was glad. She'd never really approved of Steve. She'd thought he was too wild and crazy for me. And she'd always hated me going out with him on his big motorbike. She'd be glad I'd found another boy.

Outside, I huddled in my coat against the sudden cold and set off up the street. I had to go to Steve. I had to explain to him about Peter.

The church bells rang clear in the frosty air. A small boy wobbled proudly up the empty road on a brand new bicycle, and coloured lights blinked on Christmas trees in the windows of all the houses.

I turned up the lane by the church and went to Steve . . .

WHEN I got there I didn't know what to say. I just stood there, for what seemed a long time, before the words came slowly and hesitantly.

I told him about Peter and how things were between us, how I hadn't meant it to happen but it had just the same. And I told him how sad and guilty I felt about it.

"I thought you were the only one for me," I said. "I didn't think I could ever feel that way about any other boy. But I do, Steve. Peter's very special to me, the same as you are . . . were . . . the same but different too . . ."

My eyes were filling with tears. I couldn't stop them.

"I mean . . . you're so different, you and Peter. The way I feel about him isn't better or stronger than how I felt about you. I don't know the words to explain. It's not that he's taken your place . . . just that he's become as important to me as you were . . . Do you understand, Steve? Please understand."

When I'd finished, I stood there with the tears running down my cheeks and the church bells clanging loud in my ears.

And then I turned and went away from there, back down the lane. I wiped away my tears, but it was a little while before they stopped stinging at my eyes.

The pale sun was bright in the blue sky, beginning to take away the frosty chill.

Suddenly everything began to seem right again. It was Christmas. At home the turkey was roasting deliciously. Around the tree were the magical parcels waiting to be opened. And Peter was coming to see me.

Steve understood. I knew he did. He wanted me to be happy.

I hurried home. Dad wasn't around so I went into the kitchen, to Mum and the lovely Christmas cooking smells.

"He hasn't been, has he?" I asked.

"Not yet. What's he like, your Peter?"

This time I could return her gaze. "Nice," I said.

She looked at me hard. I found myself smiling. She nodded, smiling too. "Yes," she said. "I think he might be. I'm happy for you, Sara. It's been a long time since . . ."

"Yes," I said.

"Come here," she said.

I went to her and she wiped at my cheek with her apron. "You've been crying. Where did you go for your walk?"

"Up by St Martin's Church. But I'm all right now."

"Good," she said. "You can't live in the past. It's time you put him behind you forever."

THE doorbell rang. "That'll be Peter," I said, running out of the kitchen.

In the hall I bumped into Dad. "What's the hurry?" he wanted to know. "Anyone would think you were expecting somebody important."

"I am," I smiled.

I opened the front door. It was Peter. He smiled at me, gazing at me with those warm blue eyes. "Hi, Sara. Merry Christmas!"

"Happy Christmas, Peter," I said.

He reached out to hold me but then he saw Dad and looked vaguely embarrassed instead. I introduced them. They shook hands and then Dad remembered an urgent job he had to do and vanished, grinning.

Peter put his arms round me and kissed me very gently on the lips. It was a beautiful kiss.

"I haven't brought you a present," he said. "I didn't know you even liked me until last night."

"You just gave me the nicest present," I said.

He looked puzzled, then smiled and kissed me again.

Mum was right. You can't live in the past. And that's where Steve was and everything we'd had together.

I'd thought no-one could take his place. After that summer afternoon when they told me he'd crashed his bike it had seemed like the end of the world for me, too. I couldn't believe I'd never see my wild, crazy, funny Steve again, couldn't believe anyone else would ever make me feel the way I'd felt about him.

For months I'd shut other people out of my life. Until Peter. I'd tried to close him out as well but I'd liked him too much. And all the emotions I'd thought I'd never feel again had started to come to life like flowers in spring. I couldn't stop them.

Now I was glad. And I was glad I'd gone out this Christmas morning to visit the grave in St Martin's churchyard and talk to Steve. Because now I was certain he understood.

You can't live in the past, however good it was. There's only the future. And for the first time since that day in summer, the future looked bright.

"What are you thinking about, Sara?" Peter asked.

I looked up into his warm blue eyes and smiled. "Nothing," I said, "except that this looks like being a really lovely Christmas."

And, at last, the church bells were silent . . .

MAKEOVER

WHEN we made over two of our readers, Louise and Pauline, we discovered that although they each found some areas of make-up quite simple, certain things had them stumped. So we spent extra time solving their problems, and hopefully between the two of them we covered enough ground to help *you* solve *your* particular make-up problem, too!

Louise's Dilemma — BLUSHER BOTHER!

As Louise found it difficult to apply blusher and face shaper we concentrated on this in her photos.

2
To shape Louise's face we used a dark shade of blusher in the hollows of her cheeks rather than a brown shader, as she has such a light skin the shader would have looked very unnatural. We told her to suck in her cheeks and brushed Rimmel Translucent Blush in Copper Rose in the resulting hollow.

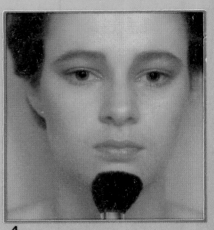

4
A little blusher on the end of her chin made her face look less long.

1
Louise, scrubbed bare of make-up! The first step to our new-look Louise was to cover the dark areas around her eyes and any skin blemishes with Rimmel Hide the Blemish (Light). Next the whole face and eyelids were covered with Max Factor Colour Fast, Soft Ivory No. 1, using a sponge, then dusted with Rimmel Loose Face Powder in Translucent Finish. The eyebrows were brushed into shape and accentuated with Yardley Nut Brown Eye Pencil, and eyes were shaped and shaded using Leichner's Box of Tricks shadows. Manhattan Skyline (a light pink) went over the whole lid, Hollywood Pink (a medium pink) was brushed in the inner corner of the eye, and Deep Purple was applied to the outer corner of the eyelid. The outer corner of the upper lid and underneath the lower lashes were accentuated with Leichner's Zoom in Purple pencil, and finally Yardley's Violet Mascara was applied to the upper and lower lashes.

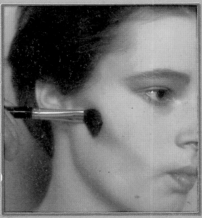

3
On top of this blusher and over the cheek went Rimmel Translucent blush in Cheeky Pink.

5
Rimmel Shimmering Highlighter went on her cheekbones, blended in well so as not to look too obvious.

M✷AGIC!

6
We outlined Louise's lips with Rimmel Cerise lip-liner pencil, then filled in the shape with Rimmel Talked About lipstick to complete her day look.

(Clothes from Richard Shops.)

7
For a special evening look, we added to her daytime make-up by applying a little Magenta Magic by Leichner to the inner corner of the eyelid, and a little of Leichner's Silver Streak shadow to the outer corner of the eyelid. Finally a touch of roll-on Rimmel Lip Gloss over her lipstick added glamour! (Louise's dress is from Richard Shops, jewellery is by Adrien Mann.)

Continued on page 26

Continued from page 25

MAKEOVER

Pauline's Problem: EYE APPEAL!

Pauline wanted to make her eyes look bigger, and she also found it difficult to buy products that suited both her skin colour and texture. So we were pleased to introduce her to Flori Roberts and Fashion Fair make-up which is specially for coloured girls.

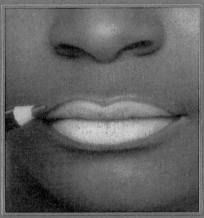

1
Pauline as she was before we set to work!

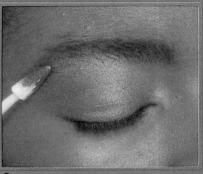

3
Then we applied Fashion Fair's Winterberry eyeshadow to the outer corner of her eyelid.

4
Max Factor's Maxi Lash mascara in Black was brushed on to her top and bottom lashes.

2
We started by concealing the dark areas around the eyes and skin blemishes with Flori Roberts Under-Cover Vanish stick (dark), then covered the whole face, including eyelids, with Flori Roberts Touche Satin Finish, using a sponge. To shape the face we placed a dark foundation shade (Brown Satin) underneath the cheekbone and down the sides of the nose, and a lighter shade (Copper Satin) down the centre of the nose and along the cheekbone. Then we powdered over Pauline's face with Fashion Fair Translucent Bronze face powder, brushed her eyebrows into shape and accentuated them with Max Factor's Maxi eyeliner pencil in Jet Black. The next step was to introduce Pauline to eye make-up and here you can see her applying Fashion Fair's Golden Chestnut eyeshadow to the inner corner of her eyelid.

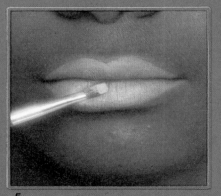

5
Pauline wanted to make her lips look thinner, so first of all we covered them entirely with Flori Roberts Under-Cover Vanish stick (dark).

6
Then we used Mary Quant's Stylewriter in Cocoa Smudge to outline the new shape.

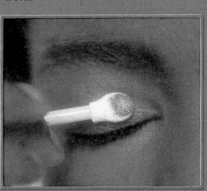

7
We filled in the new outline with Fashion Fair's Chocolate Sherry lipstick.

➡️

9
For a more glamorous look for a special night out we applied a little Miners Soft Eye Stix in blue to the inner edge of the lower eyelid, and drew a fine line with Max Factor's Eye Colour Duo Pencil (Ocean Light) along the upper lids of her eyes close to her lashes. We coloured the tips of her lashes with Outdoor Girl's mascara in navy blue and Rimmel's Golden Gloss lip gloss slicked over her lips added the final touch! (Pauline's dress is from Lady at Lord John and her jewellery from Adrien Mann and Corocraft.)

MAGIC!

8
We added some Flori Roberts Vermillion blusher to her cheeks and some Apri-Gleam highlighter on top of her cheekbones and her day look was complete! (Pauline's top is by Honeysuckle and her skirt from Lady at Lord John.)

HORSING AROUND!

SHE LOOKS NICE. I WONDER WHAT SHE'S DOING OUT HERE ALL BY HERSELF? AND LOOKING SO SAD, TOO.

She brightened up when she saw me, though.

Hello! What are you doing wandering about here on your own?

I WAS JUST ABOUT TO ASK YOU THE SAME THING, MY DEAR.

Come on. I'll give you some grass and then we'll see about getting you home.

GRASS AND A CUDDLE FROM A PRETTY GIRL, THIS IS MY LUCKY DAY.

I soon discovered why she was so sad.

Did you know that all boys—yourself excepted, of course —are creeps?

TELL ME MORE, MY DEAR.

So she did . . .

HE BRINGS ME TO A PARTY —THEN STARTS TO CHAT UP SOMEONE ELSE!

I'm not having a very good time, Dave. I'd like to go home.

Suit yourself. There's a bus stop on the corner.

Then there was Scott.

So I'll see you tomorrow, then.

Yes, Scott.

But . . .

HE'S NOT GOING TO TURN UP. WHY DID HE SAY HE'D SEE ME AGAIN WHEN HE OBVIOUSLY DIDN'T WANT TO . . .

The next boy she liked a lot. But he went away to college.

I'll write to you, Alison. I promise.

He didn't, of course. So the fact is, you're the nicest guy I've met in a long time.

AND YOU'RE THE BEST CUDDLER I'VE MET.

Then, of course, what's-his-face had to come along

Hoi! Stop stuffing that pony with grass! He's fat enough as it is!

CHARMING! YOU CAN ALWAYS COUNT ON ANDY, MY BOSS, TO MESS THINGS UP.

You little pest, Fred! I've told you before about wandering out of the stable on your own!

Pest, is he? Well, if that's how you treat him, no wonder the poor thing tries to escape!

What?

THAT'S RIGHT. YOU TELL HIM, ALISON.

Not that it's any of your business, but let me tell you that Fred here lives like a lord. All he has to do for a living is give little kids rides. I wish I had it as easy!

But she hadn't finished . . .

That's how YOU say you treat him! He probably thinks differently! I may just report you to the RSPCA before I'm finished!

She stalked off in a right state.

Who was that, Fred? And how could you just stand there and let her think I was some kind of monster?

OH, IT WAS EASY, REALLY. MY NATURAL ACTING ABILITY.

She was nice, though. I could quite fancy her. Pity we couldn't have met under different circumstances.

IT WOULDN'T HAVE DONE YOU ANY GOOD, MATE. SHE'S OFF BOYS AT THE MOMENT. SHE LIKES SWEET LITTEL PONIES, THOUGH.

He was a bit quiet over the next few days.

Time to get saddled up, Fred. The kids'll be here soon.

NO CHEERFUL GOOD MORNING. MOST STRANGE.

He seemed to be in a daze half the time.

Andy! Where are you going with Fred? There are no rides this morning!

What? Oh, yes, sorry, Boss. I forgot . . .

Not only that, but he left me outside the wrong stall. I didn't mind that, though . . .

AT LEAST I'M NEXT TO LUCY. THE MOST BEAUTIFUL PONY IN THE WHOLE WORLD. IT MAKES MY MANE CURL EVERY TIME I SEE HER.

Then Dreamy Dan appeared.

HO!! YOU'RE PUTTING MY SADDLE ON THE WRONG WAY ROUND! AND IN FRONT OF LUCY, TOO! SHE MUST THINK I'M A RIGHT TWIT TO HAVE YOU AS A BOSS!

I decided enough was enough. So next time he left me alone . . .

I'VE GOT TO FIND ALISON AGAIN. IF I CAN GET ANDY AND HER TOGETHER, MAYBE THINGS WILL GET BACK TO NORMAL.

I found her in the same place I'd first come across her.

Fred! Have you escaped again?

I DON'T ESCAPE, MY DEAR. I MERELY WALK OUT OF THE YARD AS THE FANCY TAKES ME.

I got a nice cuddle again.

I feel terrible, Fred. A friend of mine told me your boss is a pretty nice guy. I'd like to apologise to him, but there's no way he'd speak to me now.

But wait a minute! I've just thought of a fantastic idea!

There! You take my ribbon back to the stables and see if Andy gets the message.

WELL, HE IS A BIT DENSE SOMETIMES, BUT I'LL CERTAINLY TRY MY BEST.

I must admit, though, I didn't go back right away.

I'LL JUST HAVE A LITTLE SNACK THEN I'LL BE ON MY WAY.

There you are!

You little schemer! I've told you before about . . . but wait a minute . . . what's this . . . ?

It's hers! The one she was wearing that day! I wonder . . . ?

Come on, Fred. I've got a little job for you.

OH, OH. I DON'T LIKE THE SOUND OF THAT. WHAT'S HE UP TO?

I soon found out . . .

Right. You go back and find Alison again. And make sure she reads this note.

Come on, no time to waste.

MAYBE NOT FOR YOU, BUT I WANTED TO STAY AND CHAT TO LUCY. HOW WILL SHE EVER KNOW HOW I FEEL ABOUT HER IF I NEVER GET A CHANCE TO TELL HER?

But work had to come first . . .

I MUST ADMIT I FEEL A BIT FOOLISH. I HOPE SHE TURNS UP SOON.

But I needn't have worried . . .

Fred? Are you alone? The ribbon didn't work then . . .

YES, YES, IT WORKED. NOW COME AND READ THE NOTE.

32

LOVE IS ALL YOU NEED...

There weren't many people who could afford a winter holiday in the sun, but my sister was one of them and I was really envious of her. It took me a while to realise that some things are more important . . .

A Reader's True Experience

STANDING with a cup of tea in my hand, and with one eye on the clock, I read the postcard again. Outside the October rain teemed against the window, making the sunny, colourful picture on the front of the card seem even more unreal.

"Having a super time. Nothing but sun, sand and gorgeous grub. Both Mike and I have tans you wouldn't believe! See you soon—love, Clare."

Oh, I would believe it, I thought to myself miserably. I could just picture my sister and her latest in a long line of fantastic boyfriends lying sunning themselves on a beach in Corfu, while I was stuck at home with the rain, school and nothing but grotty O-levels staring me in the face.

"Seeing Tim tonight?" Mum asked, coming into the kitchen and breaking into my thoughts.

"Probably," I sighed, knowing I would.

"He's a nice lad, your Tim," she said carefully, looking at me.

"Mm." I knew what she meant. Sometimes I think my mum has X-ray eyes, especially where Clare and me are concerned.

As soon as I got to class, I showed my friend Avril the card, knowing she'd be impressed. And she was. "Lucky devil," she sighed enviously.

"I know." I put the card back in my bag and heaved a sigh to match her own. "Sometimes it just doesn't seem worth staying on for O-levels, does it? Especially when you think how well Clare's done for herself. I mean, a buyer at Riddell's, at nineteen! Look what she earns!"

"Enough for winter holidays in the sun, for starters," Avril said moodily. "When's she due back, anyway?"

"Tomorrow morning," I replied.

Tim would just never be like Mike, I thought, as I went off to my first lesson. He'd never make a car salesman; he was tongue-tied just meeting someone new. I tried to stifle the irritation I could feel rising up inside me, but I couldn't. It built up and up, and when Tim came over to join me at lunch, as he always did, I couldn't stop myself picking a fight with him.

"All this because you're jealous of your sister, Bev," he said exasperatedly. "Well, if you're not going to be good company, I'm off to find someone who will!" And he picked up his lunch tray and marched off.

He didn't wait for me after school, and he didn't come round that night, either, but I didn't really care. I just went on feeling miserable, hung around the house all evening and went to bed early.

I didn't feel much better when I got up next morning, though a weak November sun was struggling to shine outside. I clumped downstairs and waited for Clare to arrive.

Right on the dot of eleven a taxi drew up and she got out. I ran to open the door and there she was, all glowing and tanned and making me feel like a white worm. I was pleased to see her, though.

"Here," she said, delving into her bag. "This is for you, Bev."

EAGERLY I ripped at the paper. It was a tiny bottle of expensive French perfume, the kind I could remember envying when she'd got a bottle for Christmas from Dave. Or was it John? No, it'd been Larry.

I put the bottle on the table and spotted her postcard. I picked it up, held it out.

"Really good post, these foreign places," I laughed. "It only came yesterday morning. Anyway—how was the holiday? And how's Mike?"

She took it from me and stared down at it for several moments, not answering.

"Clare?" I said tentatively. "Clare? What's up?"

"Finished," she said, almost inaudibly. "Mike and me—all washed up."

"Oh Clare," I put my arms round her shoulder. "I'm sorry. But it happens, you've said so yourself. There'll be someone new."

She turned then, and the expression in her eyes almost made me step back. I'd never seen her look so unhappy.

"Oh, Bev," she said, her voice wobbling in the effort to control it. "What's wrong with me? What? It's always so super, so right, and I always think—this time it's got to be it. This time it'll be like you and Tim."

I stared at her, trying to get my muddled thoughts into some sort of order.

"Like *us?* Me and Tim?"

She nodded. "I'd give anything to be like you, Bev. You always know where you're going and who with. You're so sure of things."

"But I thought—" I began. And then I stopped. What had I thought? And how wrong could you be, even about your own sister and what went on in her head?

Mum came back then and Clare immediately shut up and gave her her present. She didn't mention Mike again to me.

I watched her and thought for the first time in my life—poor old Clare. It was odd, thinking that. Odder to think she actually envied me—me, of all people!

The phone rang then, and I saw her eyes fill with sudden hope as Mum went to answer it. But it was Tim.

"I'm sorry, Bev," he kept saying, over and over. "I'm really sorry."

I knew it was me who ought to be saying that. I kept trying to tell him so but he wouldn't listen. I knew I'd make it up to him, though, make him see that it didn't matter, nothing did as long as we had each other. That was the important thing.

"I'm coming over right now," I said. As I put the phone down I could hear Clare talking in a quick, over-bright voice.

Funny now to think I'd really believed she had everything.

As I ran upstairs to get my jacket, I hoped she'd find someone like Tim soon. Someone who she really deserved, someone she could truly love.

And then, I knew, she'd be just as lucky as I was . . .

33

THE SITUATION

You walk into your bedroom one day to find your mum deeply into your most SECRET DIARY, with an expression of shocked horror on her face and steam coming out of her ears. So . . .

DON'T SAY *"Oh no, you can't trust anybody nowadays, what's the meaning of privacy if people can come barging into your room whenever you're out for a few seconds and go snooping around among your most private possessions? Who do you think you are anyway – M.I.5?"*

DO SAY *"Ah — I'm glad to see you're reading my latest English Literature project. It's called, 'Diary of an Incurable Liar.'"*

THE SITUATION

Your boyfriend said he was going to a night-school class, so when you bump into gorgeous Gary and he starts to chat you up, you count your blessings and stroll in an intimate way with him towards the chippie — when lo and behold, who should pop up but your boyfriend, with a face like thunder. So . . .

DON'T SAY *"Crikey, Martin, I didn't expect you to be – er – I mean I thought you were – that is, this is my cousin Rolf from Australia, um, can't you see the family resemblance . . .er . . . ?"*

DO SAY *"Hey, Mart, this is Gary. I was just telling him about you. What a coincidence — tell him about your motorbike, I couldn't remember the gory details . . ."*

DON'T SAY THAT—SAY THIS!

Do you envy those people who always seem to be able to get themselves out of embarrassing, awkward situations with just a few well-chosen words? Where you would stand mumbling and going bright red, they keep their cool and manage to pass the whole thing off as a joke.

Their secret, of course, is that they know how to say the RIGHT THING. So take a look at some embarrassing, awkward situations and learn what to say and what *not* to say . . .

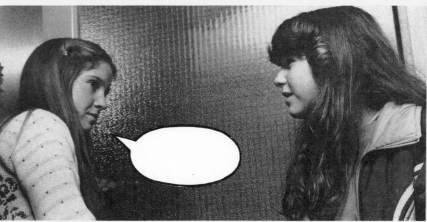

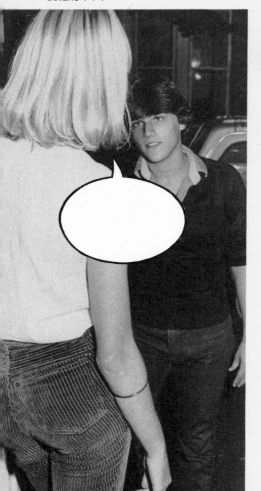

THE SITUATION

You've promised your mum that you won't smoke any more. But there you were, idly lounging about blowing smoke-rings at the ceiling, thinking she was out shopping, when you hear her unmistakable step in the hall and POW! the door's flung open and you're caught. So . . .

DON'T SAY *"Oh dear, how stupid, I just wasn't thinking. I didn't really mean to, I was just sort of in a daze. I can't think what's wrong with me lately, perhaps all this smoking has destroyed some of my brain cells . . ."*

DO SAY *"Do you know, the oddest thing just happened. There I was, wondering what to buy you for your birthday, when a man came in the window, shoved this lighted cigarette in my hand and then ran away laughing. I wonder who he was? Any ideas?"*

THE SITUATION

While your best friend was away on holiday, you enjoyed your nights at the disco in a very special way — with her boyfriend, Steve. Now she's back and somebody's told her, and she lands on your doorstep like a paper bag full of hornets. So . . .

DON'T SAY *"Dance with Dave? What, **me**? Dave Who? I may have done, I can't quite remember . . . let's see, what did I do? . . . Washed my hair. . .went to the launderette . . . read "Wuthering Heights" . . . then . . . oh yes maybe I did, at least, I danced with **somebody**, and I suppose it **might** have been Dave . . ."*

DO SAY *"Did I dance with Dave? Of course I did. If I hadn't kept him out of the way, Vampy Valerie would've got her claws into him and that's the last you'd have seen of him, ever!"*

THE SITUATION

You're having a quiet cuddle with your boyfriend on the sofa when the phone rings . . . and help! It's the guy you met on holiday, and you've been hoping and praying he'll ring . . . and he wants to have a smoochy conversation with you, but your boyfriend can overhear every word, and when you get back to the sofa, he gives you one of the blackest looks since Rasputin. So . . .

DON'T SAY "Who was that? . . . Listen, what is this? The Interviewing room at Scotland Yard? What's it to you anyway who rings me up? And anyway, he was a creep. And anyway, he wanted to talk to my brother really, so there!"

DO SAY "What a *bore*! If I ever have to talk to that guy again I'll get the screaming abdabs! Why didn't you rescue me by imitating a kettle boiling over or something? Honestly, you're so USELESS!"

THE SITUATION

You and your boyfriend are enjoying a not-so-quiet little cuddle on the sofa when your parents come back unexpectedly early. They burst into the sitting-room and there you both are, wrapped round each other on the sofa. So . . .

DON'T SAY "Oh, Mum – Agh, Dad – it's not what you think . . . We were just . . . I mean, Dave was just going . . .

that is, Dave's not like that . . . we were just . . . Dave isn't that sort of guy . . ."

DO SAY "Hey, great to see you! Was your evening awful? Has Mum got one of her headaches? Dave's learned this terrific sort of Chinese massage that's just great for headaches! He just got rid of my migraine — sit down and let him try it out on you, Mum!"

THE SITUATION

You've skived off school to go round the shops with your mate. You're sure it'll be safe because your mum's got a coffee morning, but heavens above, who should you see across the T-shirts at Top Shop but your very own mum — looking at you with her very own, very famous expression of amazement and shock. So . . .

DON'T SAY "Mum! What are you doing here? You should be at your coffee morning! It's been really strange – you see, on my way to school I felt ill, so I started to come home, then about half-way there I started to feel better, so I started to go back, then I met Penny on her way back from the dentist, and she felt a bit faint so we thought we'd come in here till she felt better . . ."

DO SAY "Hey, Mum! We're doing this project — it's great — we have to go round the shops and interview shoppers. Can we interview you first? Now, are you an impulse buyer, or do you always have a list . . . ?"

THE SITUATION

It's your first date with the incredibly gorgeous Charley Black, and horrors! you're late. You can't decide what to wear, you miss the bus, and finally arrive twenty minutes late and out of breath. Charley is looking more than a little ratty. So . . .

DON'T SAY "Oh gosh, I'm sorry – don't think I'm like this always – oh, you didn't think I'd stood you up, did you? I'd never dream of it, honestly, I'm just so hopelessly disorganised – are you really mad with me? – please speak to me, say you're not mad at me, please, Charley, don't look at me like that, it's awful . . ."

DO SAY "Sorry about that. Got held up.

Old woman knocked over in the street. Had to give her first aid and call the police and all that stuff. Don't really want to talk about it any more. Sorry, anyway. Let's go in."

THE SITUATION

IT'S HAPPENED! You've *forgotten your mum's birthday*! And after she dropped so many hints, too! And after your dad reminded you three times! You're covered with shame and Mum's trying to pretend not to care. So . . .

DON'T SAY "Well, birthdays aren't every-thing, are they? Especially at your age, eh, Mum? I mean, you're not as young as you were – I thought the kindest thing would just be to forget them from now on, eh?"

DO SAY "Ah, Mum, you're too important for a mere ordinary birthday — you're going to have an official birthday instead like the Queen, and it's going to be a big surprise for you. I'm organising the whole thing, it might just be ready by tomorrow!"

THE SITUATION

Your mum's lost patience with your promises to tidy your room, so she's sent you upstairs with strict instructions to have it all cleaned up in one hour. You start clearing up, but discover your old records and old diaries and start to look through them. An hour later, your mum comes in and *nothing's been done*. She's breathing fire and building up to a rage. So . . .

DON'T SAY "How do you expect me to start tidying my room when you keep barging in to check up on me? And you said an hour and it's only been fifteen minutes! It's just not fair! I'm going out!"

DO SAY "Oh no, it can't be that time already! I've been so engrossed in my diary. Do you know, Mum, last year I wrote in my diary that I spent so much time doing my homework and visiting old ladies and sick cats, that I just didn't have time to tidy my room. But this year it's going to be different. The old ladies and cats will just have to look after themselves as best they can. This year, my room comes first."

35

Dear Angela

A Reader's True Experience

15 Avonscourt Road,
Bellshill.

Dear Angela,

I know I have to write this letter, to apologise for last night, and to explain why I did what I did. Every time I think of the way you looked when you found out, I feel I have to tell you I'm sorry — so very sorry.

You see, I'd been crazy about Lorraine for ages — everyone seemed to know it. We'd been going out together for close on three months — a record for her. I was never really sure of her, I never knew quite where I stood with her from one minute to the next. And then, as you know — as everyone knows — she finished with me.

I was shattered. I couldn't seem to think straight — couldn't think of anything at all except her. And that's when my mate Sam said to me, "Look, Mark, the only way you're going to get her back is to make her jealous. Go out with someone else. If she's got any interest left in you at all, she'll come running. Tell you what — ask Angela Harris, she's never out with anyone."

He said exactly that, Angela. It was yesterday morning, Saturday, and we were in town as usual, just going into Carlo's Café on the High Street. I saw you in there with some of your friends, showing each other what you'd bought. You were just showing Rosemary Fallon your new T-shirt when I came up.

I took hold of a corner of the shirt and grinned. "That's nice," I said. "Are you going to the disco in it tonight?"

You blushed, grabbed the top out of my fingers and bundled it back into its white polythene bag. "I don't know," you answered, not looking at me.

"Let's put it another way," I said. "Will you? With me?"

You just nodded, still not looking at me, your brown silky hair waving to and fro, your face still scarlet. But I could tell you were pleased.

"I'll see you in there, then," I promised, being cool — not letting on that I was pleased too — and left you to your girl-talk. While Sam and I sat at the other side of the café, I could see that your friends were teasing you about your date.

We were at the disco early — and you were there already. You were wearing jeans and your new pink top — and your face went nearly the same colour when you saw me.

"You came, then," you stammered, with a shy smile.

"Sure I came," I replied, anxious to put you at ease. "What are you drinking?"

"Oh — anything. Coke?"

I caught you by the hand and pulled you to the bar with me. "Let's leave your friends," I murmured. "More than two's a crowd." Then it struck me that I really wanted to make sure that Lorraine, when she arrived, would be in no doubt that we were together.

Then she walked in. I was aware of her almost immediately. She stood by the door, making sure she was seen, her long legs made longer by the short, her thick, dark flared skirt she wore, her hair tumbling in curls over her shoulders.

You were telling me about your dog at the time, and I had to drag my attention back to you.

"And he's only got to see a stranger to roll over on his back and have his tummy tickled," you smiled.

"A lot of use he'd be if a burglar broke in, eh?" I joked, keeping one eye on Lorraine.

"That's just what we always say!" Your face shone.

You really came out of your shell, didn't you, Angela? And as the evening passed, you seemed to grow in confidence. You even told me how much you were enjoying yourself while we were dancing.

"You've stopped being shy," I said.

You went pink. "I've not been out with that many boys," you explained.

"Because you're shy?"

You nodded. "It's stupid, isn't it? Boys have asked me — and I've just said no, without even giving myself time to think about it."

"I don't think it's stupid," I replied then. "I think it's nice." And I really meant it, Angela. I wasn't just feeding you a line. "But you didn't say no to me," I added.

I was mad about Lorraine and wanted her back, so I used you, Angela, to make her jealous. And now I'm regretting it . . .

You looked away. "I've liked you for a long time, Mark," you said, so quietly I almost didn't catch it. And I was pleased — more pleased than I thought I could be, especially since it took a full ten minutes for you to pluck up the courage to look at me again.

I became so absorbed in our conversation that I forgot all about Lorraine. But Sam hadn't. He came charging up to me when you'd gone to the loo for a moment, and I was cooling off in the corridor outside, waiting for you.

"Hey, Mark, it's working!" he hailed me excitedly. "Lorraine's just been asking me all these questions about the girl you're with — who is she, how long have you known her, is it serious! I tell you, her eyes have gone green, mate! You've only got to click your fingers and she'll jump!"

When he was speaking, I could feel that stupid grin spreading all over my face. And then it faded. I had seen what he, standing with his back to the door, couldn't possibly see — you standing in the doorway, taking in every jubilant word . . .

You came out slowly, and walked straight past me.

"Angela," I began, catching your arm. But you shook me off, and stared at me with those brilliant green eyes as cold as marble. "It doesn't matter, Mark," you said in an even voice. "Your plan's worked — you don't need to pretend to me any more. I thought it was too good to be true — I'm glad I could be of some assistance . . ."

And then you turned and dashed back into the disco and out of sight; but not before I'd seen your tears.

I felt rotten. For a long time I just stood there, looking after you, not knowing what to do. And then Sam took my arm and steered me towards Lorraine. As soon as she saw me, she flung her arms round my neck.

"Mark, it's great to see you!" She turned her face up to mine, and I could see that Sam was right — she was jealous. I even felt quite elated for a while — after all, that was the plan, and it had worked . . .

She dragged me on to the dance floor, clinging on to me possessively and telling me all about what she'd been doing lately — going to parties and dating boys, mostly. And then, suddenly, I don't really know how it happened, I found that I wasn't elated any more. In fact I was almost bored.

Lorraine's conversation was all about herself, and it was pretty plain that she wasn't really interested in me as a person — just possessive about me when she thought I was going out with someone else. In fact, Lorraine, I realised suddenly, could never be interested in anyone but herself. Then I thought of you, telling me about your dog and your family, your hopes and fears, and admitting how shy you were. And I knew that that must have taken courage.

I stood away from Lorraine and looked round for you. I could see your friends, but you were nowhere about.

Lorraine followed my eyes. "Where's that girl you were with, Mark?"

"Gone, I think."

"She wasn't important to you then," she said, coming up to me and putting her arms round my neck again. It wasn't really a question, more like a statement — and I realised that she expected me just to drop everything and come running because *she* wanted it.

"Well, since you ask —" I freed her arms from my neck. "She was more important to me than I thought."

And I walked out, away from her, away from Sam, who wanted to know what I was playing at, away from everything. I looked for you in the street — in fact I walked all the way to your house in the hope of catching you up and explaining what I'm telling you here. But I didn't catch you, which is why I'm writing this letter.

I had to say I'm sorry, and to explain, and to ask — will you go out with me properly? I'll understand if you want to say no, but if you will, I'll be so happy. Because you do mean so much to me.

I'll be in Carlo's at ten on Monday. Please be there,
All my love,

Mark

Carlo's Café,
12 High Street,
Bellshill.

Dear Emilia,
You know, a funny thing happened in my café today. There I was, wiping down the counter top, when this girl rushes in, waving this paper. It looked like a letter, or something. And then this bloke leaps up from his chair, knocks over his coffee, all over the place, and runs to her and gives her an enormous hug. Right there, in front of everyone! Well, I don't know what my regulars thought, but it was quite sweet, really. Pretty girl, too. Brown hair and amazing green eyes.
Well, anyway . . .

D'YOU FEUD WITH YOUR FOLKS?

D'you spell trouble, driving your folks frantic with your funny friends and frowning face – or are you the angel of the family, inviting your fella round for cucumber sandwiches with Mum? Try our quiz and see if you're playing at happy families!

A Jackie Quiz

1. Your brother's been dying to see his favourite team play at the weekend, but when you announce that you'll need a hand to cart Mum's shopping home, it seems his football plans are out of the window. Does he:

a. *cast his striped scarf into the cupboard with a smile – there's always next week, after all – and cheerfully offer to help you,*

b. *throw a tantrum and remind you about the five hundred other times you've spoilt his fun, then pelt off to his room with a slam of the door,*

c. *shrug and offer to help – after you've twisted his arm 360 degrees,*

d. *willingly offer to carry the shopping 'cos it's too heavy for you – and he doesn't want you injuring yourself?*

2. Your mum's spent ages baking a huge, elaborate cake for your birthday, using her favourite recipe — the one that brings you out in a lumpy rash! Do you:

d. *snap, "Yeuch!" and help yourself to the trifle,*

c. *cut yourself a wafer-thin slice, concealing most of it under the tablecloth,*

a. *cheerfully hack away a huge chunk – what's a silly little rash compared with hurting your mum's feelings,*

b. *throw your slice at the dog?*

3. Mum and Dad are going away for the week, leaving you in your gran's care. Is your reaction:

b. oh no – I was going to hold wild parties every night and redecorate my room,

a. great – I love Gran's cooking and she might even teach me how to knit,

c. oh well – it's only for a week, and I'll still be able to go out on Friday night,

d. WAAAGH! – punctuated with a few sobs and a lot of stamping of the feet?

4. You're getting ready for a night at the disco. Your face is scrubbed and you're poised ready to slap on the warpaint, when you notice that your lipstick's mashed to a pulp and everything's covered with foundation. Do you:

c. hold your tongue till you find out who it is – then growl and grumble,

d. whimper to your mum about your make-up being ruined – and beg her to buy you a new lot,

a. shrug and clear up the mess, doing as best a job as you can with what's left,

b. fling your gunged-up articles into your sister's make-up bag – and nick her nice, new stuff?

5. You're tying yourself in knots with your algebra homework, and when Dad offers to help, you're not so sure that he's got it right, either. Do you:

c. scribble down Dad's answer to the question anyway – he probably **is** right,

d. shove your book on to Dad's lap and snarl, "If you're so clever, do the whole chapter!",

a. confidently jot down Dad's answer – he's **always** right,

b. decide to forget about the homework and play your records instead?

6. Your sister's had her hair done in a new style — all blonde and frizzy. You're not too impressed, though, and when she asks what you think, do you:

d. laugh in her face and tell her how awful she looks,

a. gush, "Oh – it's gorgeous! I'll have mine done just like it!",

b. chuckle and make a joke about lawn-mowers,

c. tell her she looks fine – you don't want to shatter her confidence?

7. There's a pile of dishes glaring at you from the draining board, and it doesn't look as if anyone's thinking of washing them up. Do you:

d. bawl at your brother to grab a dishcloth and get scrubbing,

a. roll up your sleeves and work your way through the lot,

b. sneak off to your mate's with an evil snigger – **you're** not doing that lot,

c. rope your sister in to help and – amid groans and grumbles – tackle the job?

8. Your mum's been constantly nagging you to bring your new fella round for tea, so that she can give him the full interrogation and poison him with her scones. Do you:

c. explain to your guy that it's only for a few hours and her sandwiches aren't **too** bad – and drag him along,

a. jump at the chance of showing off your folks to your fella – you might even be able to have a sing-song round the piano,

d. stamp your foot and sulk till they drop the idea,

b. persuade him to dye his hair pink, wear odd socks and ripped jeans – **then** take him to meet Mummy?

9. Your big brother barges in when you're having a snuggle with your boyfriend, and insists on telling your guy all about your nervous twitch and smelly feet. Do you:

b. reply with a lurid description of your brother's rash – accompanied by photographs in full colour,

d. burst into tears,

c. drag your fella off to the disco and leave your brother to natter on by himself,

a. make your brother a cuppa and introduce them – they might as well be mates?

10. What would you miss most if — gasp! — your parents went off on their hols and left you alone in the house?

a. Someone to talk things over with.

b. Miss them? You'd be too busy holding parties every night!

d. Someone to wash your clothes, vacuum your room, make your bed...

c. Your mum's flaky pastry.

11. Your beloved puppy, Custer, has run amok and uprooted Dad's prize plants. When Dad announces that it's Custer's last stand — that Custer has to go — do you:

c. have a secret snivel and decide to save up for another pup,

d. throw a tantrum in the garden, uprooting the rest of Dad's plants,

a. accept that he's been a bad puppy and that you can't have a wild animal going beserk in the garden,

b. smuggle Custer round to your mate's – together with a supply of doggie chocs – and tell your dad that yes, Custer's been taken away?

12. Finally, how many of the following situations couldn't you bear? A picnic with Granny and a selection of aunts. Your mum meeting you outside the school gates. A drive in the country in your dad's new car. Tackling the housework with Mum. Sharing your clothes with an unruly little sis.

b. Most of them – you'd die of embarrassment!

c. A few of them – housework isn't **that** bad, though.

a. None of them – you **love** picnics.

d. All of them – you wouldn't be seen dead with a member of your family!

So, are you the darling of the family — or d'you make Mum yearn for the safety of her kitchen? Add up your score — mostly a's, b's, c's or d's — look at the conclusions and all will be revealed!

Conclusions

Mostly a's

Lucky family, that's all we can say! *You're* not likely to keep them waiting, frantic with worry, counting the flowers on the wallpaper while you dance away at the disco! Nope, you'd much rather spend your evenings tackling homework — in between doing the vacuuming, of course, and being the perfect, model daughter. Unless, of course, they get a little tired of "yes, Mum, no, Dad, of course, dear brother!"

Mostly b's

What? You can't be serious, can you — are you *really* as unruly as this? Your poor distraught folks — you certainly drive them up the wall, and there's an element of fun in your mischievous nature that's likely to leave your family in a state of total confusion! Mum'll be shouting at sis, brother'll be roaring at Dad — meanwhile, you'll have plonked yourself in front of the telly, leaving them to it!

Mostly c's

Well done — you've achieved a pretty healthy balance — you're neither the angel of the family nor the terror! You're willing to muck in and do your share, although like most of us you'd rather be listening to records — and things at your place probably run pretty smoothly — 99 per cent, of the time, anyway! Carry on just the way you are and you'll be pretty popular where your family are concerned!

Mostly d's

Aaagh — not another tantrum! We reckon your family have either developed nerves of steel or have given up altogether — as you clam up and that petted lip protrudes once again! Hardly the angel of the family, are you? As far as you're concerned, you don't see why you *should* lend a hand at home — after all, what are mums for, if it's not doing the washing, the cooking, the cleaning, the vacuuming, the bed-making . . .

39

WHAT DO BOYS

Your reaction to each of the scenes below can tell you an awful lot about your attitude to boys—and can also reveal what *they* think about *you*. Just pick which sentence you think best fits each scene, add up your score and then turn to the conclusions to find out just what you and boys think about each other!

1. This couple have just met at a lively, fun party. Is he saying to her—
a) " OK, I give up. If that's not a jelly-baby hanging from your ear, then what is it?"
b) " Just a bit higher and you'll feel my heart beating."
c) " You must go to the same dentist as me. I can tell by your fillings."

3. She's just opened the door to this boy. What do you think he's saying to her?
a) " Is your sister in?"
b) " Remember me? We got engaged last night!"
c) " If your mum's in, I've come about the gas leak. If she's not, what are you doing tonight?"

2. These two are on their first date and he's just given her flowers. Is she saying to him—
a) " Very nice. Why have you given them to me?"
b) " They're lovely. No-one's ever given me flowers before."
c) " Thanks very much. But just *what* am I going to do with flowers in a *disco?*"

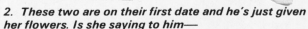

4. This couple have just finished a fun game of tennis. Is he saying to her—
a) " I don't care who won. As far as I'm concerned, it's love all."
b) " Never mind. You might win next time."
c) " You may not be very good at tennis, but at least you're game for a laugh!"

THINK OF YOU?

5. *These two are out for a romantic walk in the country. Is she saying to him—*
a) " If youre going to kiss me, do it quick before this wind blows us both away!"
b) " I never noticed before, but now I can see your eyes aren't really blue at all."
c) " I don't care what the view's like from up here. I only have eyes for you."

6. *This couple are out for a walk in the park. Is he saying to her—*
a) " Look! There goes Concorde!"
b) " We'll have a place like this one day."
c) "You and that duck have a lot in common. Neither of you are very good swimmers!"

7. *These two are fooling about with a camera. Is she saying to him—*
a) " Make sure you get in *all* my fillings, won't you!"
b) " Do you know we'll get cramp standing like this?"
c) " This photo will always remind you of me."

8. *This couple are in a disco and for a dare, she's just ripped his shirt off. Is he now saying to her—*
a) " Careful! My mum wahed that this morning!"
b) " Thanks! I neeed that! It's really hot in here!"
c) " Hey! Don't be daft! That girl *was* my cousin, you know!"

Now count up your score and turn to the conclusions.

1. a)11	b)9	c)7.
2. a)7	b)9	c)11.
3. a)7	b)9	c)11.
4. a)9	b)7	c)11.
5. a)11	b)7	c)9.
6. a)7	b)9	c)11.
7. a)11	b)7	c)9.
8. a)7	b)11	c)9.

CONCLUSIONS

IF YOU SCORED: BETWEEN 72 AND 88

You're warm, friendly and a bundle of laughs and you refuse to take anyone, far less boys, seriously. At the moment, you don't want to be tied down to one particular person. Boys like you because they feel they can talk to you easily and have a few laughs without it all getting too heavy. When you do find your particular person, though, it'll be a case of " till death us do part " because underneath all that bouncy humour, you're very loyal and sincere. Watch you don't miss out on the right boy for you, though, by being too jokey. If you are, he may think you don't care enough about him. You can be romantic and serious when you want, so give it a try sometimes!

IF YOU SCORED: BETWEEN 64 and 72

Aah! You're nothing but a big soppy romantic who wants everybody to take care of her. You're ready to fall for any boy who says two nice words to you (like, " Hi there!") and after three dates you're dreaming about engagement rings and wedding bells. Fortunately, you've got a good sense of humour which saves you taking yourself too seriously. Boys find you warm and easy to get on with, and you'll never be short of dates and admirers. Try not to see every boy you meet as the Great love of Your Life, though. If you do, boys will get scared off by your attitude and the next time you mention weddings or engagements, you won't see them for dust!

IF YOU SCORED: BETWEEN 56 AND 64

You're extremely practical and down-to-earth, but as far as boys are concerned, you're inclined to take everything they say with two pinches of salt! Maybe you've been badly hurt in the past, which would account for you being almost deliberately unromantic most of the time. This attitude does tend to scare boys off a bit because they think you don't like them. The truth is, though, you do like them—it's just that you're scared to show your feelings in case you get hurt. Maybe you should try relaxing more. Not all boys are as bad as you think. In fact, quite a few of them are very nice, if only you'll give them the chance to prove it!

41

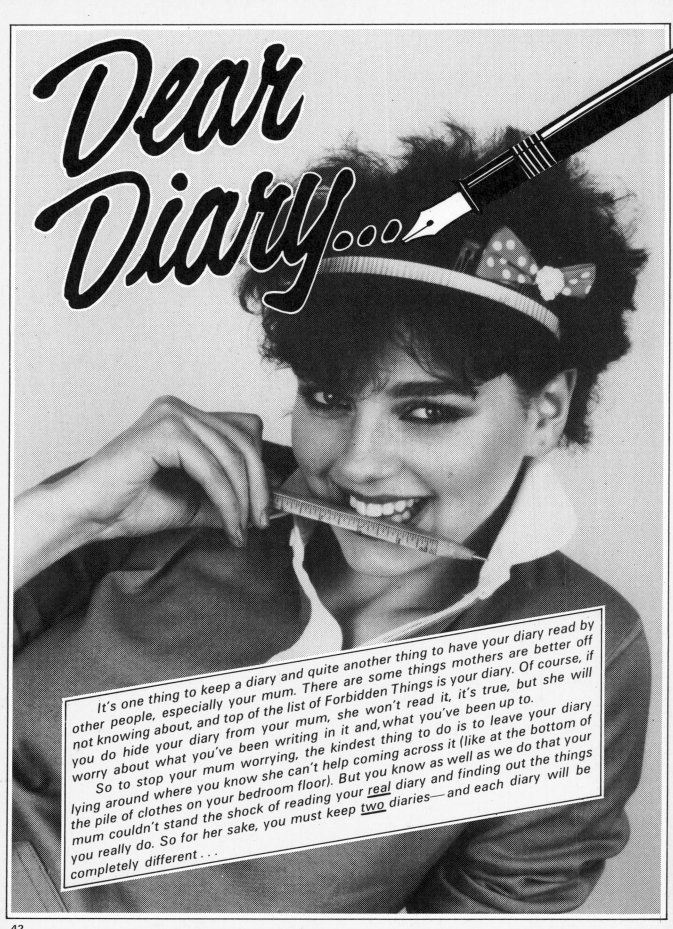

Dear Diary...

It's one thing to keep a diary and quite another thing to have your diary read by other people, especially your mum. There are some things mothers are better off not knowing about, and top of the list of Forbidden Things is your diary. Of course, if you do hide your diary from your mum, she won't read it, it's true, but she will worry about what you've been writing in it and, what you've been up to.

So to stop your mum worrying, the kindest thing to do is to leave your diary lying around where you know she can't help coming across it (like at the bottom of the pile of clothes on your bedroom floor). But you know as well as we do that your mum couldn't stand the shock of reading your _real_ diary and finding out the things you really do. So for her sake, you must keep _two_ diaries—and each diary will be completely different . . .

THE ALL-NIGHT PARTY . . .
What Really Happened.

ARRIVED at John's around 8.30 p.m. His mum and dad had gone to Yarmouth for the weekend and while the cat's away . . . The music was so loud you could hear it three streets away, and when I arrived, there was already somebody lying under the rhododendrons in the front garden.

John had dyed his hair in honour of the occasion, and Marilyn welcomed us by shaking a can of shandy and letting it off all over the room. Seven of us got soaked so we went upstairs and had a shower together—without taking our clothes off! Then we danced for two hours to dry off. It was fantastic—the neighbours only complained three times.

Finally I crashed out at about 4 a.m. under the stairs. It was a bit cramped—I had to share my corner with the Crumhorn twins, fat Eileen, John's dog and John's dad's golfclubs. I woke up to find the golfclubs on fire—fat Eileen had been smoking in her sleep. We put 'em out by throwing an old rug on top of them. John went a bit pale when he saw the mess, but we were all a bit pale by then.

Had three aspirins for breakfast and limped home on the shady side of the street.

THE ALL-NIGHT PARTY . . .
Version For Mum To Read.

ARRIVED at Jane's at 8.30 p.m. Her mum and dad had gone to a lot of trouble making sandwiches, etc., for us and when we arrived they retired to their room in the attic with a good book, a Thermos and some earplugs. Not that the music was that loud and anyway, no-one much wanted to dance. Instead, we all sat around and talked about how to be nicer to our parents.

Jane looked fantastic—her mum had made her a lovely cotton frock—and Marilyn didn't come, which was great, 'cos she always ruins things by going too far. The party was beginning to drag by 10 p.m. so Jane's mum came downstairs and taught us all to Twist 'n' Shout. Only we didn't shout much ('cos of the neighbours).

Round about midnight Jane's mum handed out sleeping bags and we all settled down—girls upstairs, boys downstairs. We had a cocoa and Jane's mum read us a bedtime story all about the French Revolution.

Up at 8, cleared up, had big breakfast and went to church.

MY FIRST DATE WITH DAVE . . .
What Really Happened.

MY FIRST date with Dave! I was so excited I couldn't sleep all night, eat all day or think of anything else. Spent 5 hours getting ready: moisturising my eyelashes, deodorising my ankles, etc. Took my tightest trousers and highest heels with me in a carrier bag and changed into them in the Ladies Loo in the Bus Station. (Didn't put 'em on at home 'cos a) Dad would've flipped, b) Can't walk more than 50 yards in 'em without cutting off my circulation and twisting both ankles.)

Dave looked scrumptious—he'd got new black leather trousers to match his jacket, and a new tattoo— ENGLAND—right across his brow. Very patriotic, is Dave. We went to see *Flashman meets Emanuelle*. Not that I saw much of it! Lost one of my little gold fish earrings in the cinema. Or perhaps Dave ate it!

Afterwards we went to Bert's caff and had fish 'n' chips. Dave had a great line in insulting jokes, but he got on Bert's nerves so much that Bert chased us out and thumped Dave over the head. Then we had a little cuddle for 1½ hours in the bus shelter, after which Dave cadged his bus fare off me.

MY FIRST DATE WITH DAVE . . .
Version For Mum To Read.

MY FIRST date with Dave—still, nothing to get worked up about. It's silly to get serious about boys at my age, so I really only think of Dave as a friend rather than a boy—even if his dad IS the Bank manager. We met at 8.30 (Dave has lots of homework 'cos he's studying for his Oxford Scholarship). I wore my usual T shirt, jeans and trainers. I prefer the casual and natural look.

Dave looked rather nice. He'd just had a haircut and his dad had bought him a new suit. We went to see BAMBI MEETS SNOW WHITE. It was ever so sad and really beautiful. We sat in the back row but Dave didn't hold my hand once—in fact he was a perfect gentleman.

Afterwards we went to Belinda's Patisserie and had coffee and cakes. Dave told me all about his interests: choral singing and flower arranging.

He walked me home and when we reached the gate he asked if he could kiss me goodnight. I let him have a peck on the cheek. I hope he doesn't go away with the idea that I'm a fast piece.

THE DAY MY PARENTS WENT TO GRANDMA'S . . .
What Really Happened.

MUM AND DAD left for Grandma's . . . fantastic! A whole day with the house to myself! Once they'd gone I put my album on at 25 decibels. Mum's decanter shattered but so what, she never uses it anyway. Went upstairs and tried all Mum's clothes on, and experimented with her make-up and perfumes.

Then got the idea of dolling up the dog in Mum's earrings, suspender belts, etc. Dog wouldn't co-operate and ran out into the street with a black lace bra wrapped around her tail.

For lunch, ate fish and chips while lying on sofa watching TV. Then dozed off and had a lovely dream that I was wrestling with six gorgeous boys in a tubfull of chocolate mousse. Woke up on the floor with chip-paper wrapped round throat. Never mind, probably good for complexion.

Decided it would be a good idea to try Ribena in my bathwater. Nice colour but afterwards armpits very sticky. In bed by time parents returned. Sheets slightly purple from Ribena but otherwise all OK.

THE DAY MY PARENTS WENT TO GRANDMA'S . . .
Version For Mum To Read.

MUM AND DAD left for Grandma's—hope I don't feel too lonely. Still, they'll be back late tonight. Did the washing-up and also dusted the cupboards, the piano, the bookshelves and the cat.

For lunch, finished off old salad in fridge. Noticed fridge a bit grimy. Poor mum's so overworked! So I cleaned it for her. In the afternoon, did my excercises, weeded the garden, and did shopping for old Mrs Smith down the road.

Found a lot of useful things lying around the house. Collected them together and put them into a box marked USEFUL THINGS. Also collected all old paper bags and ironed them.

At 7, made supper—beans on toast. Careful not to cut finger on tin or burn mouth on beans. Chewed each mouthful 20 times—counted it—to make time pass till Mum and Dad came home. At 8.30 went to bed, read Winnie the Pooh, said my prayers and went to sleep. Dreamt I married Prince Edward.

Not To Be Sniffed At!

How to make sense out of scents!

D^o *you have a favourite perfume? Or do you make do with whatever you're given as presents? It takes time to discover the right perfume for you but it's fun finding out!*

THE HUNT BEGINS!

You could discover your favourite perfume without setting foot in a shop! That's if you fall in love with the perfume someone else is wearing. This isn't a bad way of discovering your favourite fragrance but don't be too disappointed if the perfume smells a bit different on you. Different skin types can affect the smell of a perfume quite dramatically. But if you're trying to choose a perfume in a store here's a quick guide to the different types of scents you'll find:

FLORALS – There are single florals like rose or lavender perfume and also floral bouquets where various flowers are blended. Florals are usually light and refreshing but they can be very sweet.
Try Roses by Yardley, Quelques Fleurs by Houbigant, Tramp by Lentheric, An Original Perfume by No. 7, Blase by Max Factor or Jontue by Revlon.

CITRUS – These are sharp, fresh and stimulating and suit people with oily skins. Try Ô de Lancome or Cavale by Fabergé.

MODERN – These combine synthetic materials with natural ones or can be completely synthetic. Usually bright and cool, they range from florals to woody or mossy categories. Try Charlie by Revlon (a floral), or these combined floral and woody ones – Cie by Shulton, Liberty by Yardley, Aviance by Prince Matchabelli or A Touch Of Class by Faberge.

ORIENTAL – Rich and exotic based on aromatic eastern woods and grasses. Try Sandalwood by Morny, Pagan by Jovan, Gingham by Innoxa or Chantilly by Houbigant.

GREEN – Like the moderns but warmer as they come from natural woods such as pine and cedar blended with mosses, ferns and grasses. Try Masumi by Coty, Courant by Helena Rubenstein, Chique by Yardley or Tigress by Fabergé.

MUSKS – Spicy with sultry overtones. Try Just Musk by Lentheric or Musk Oil by Jovan.

SCENTS AND CENTS!

Before you go and fall in love with something like Chanel No. 5 find out the price! Be sensible and if you want to wear a fragrance every day pick one you can splash on liberally without worrying about the cost, like one of Boots or Yardley's big bottles of cologne. Then for special occasions you can wear a more expensive scent.

Don't keep perfume for too long once you've opened the bottle as it immediately begins to evaporate. However, you can preserve your perfume a little longer by keeping it in a cool dark place rather than displayed on your dressing-table.

If you're travelling abroad for your summer hols, or know someone who is, try to discover if you like any of the perfumes likely to be sold in the duty-free shop, then you can buy your supplies there and save at least a couple of pounds.

And remember, if you can't afford your favourite fragrance as a perfume go for the Eau de Toilette or cologne, instead.

TESTING TIMES!

Once you've homed in on the type of perfume you fancy you can begin the lengthy process of testing them out on the inside of your wrists. Only do two at a time, one on each wrist, using the testers provided on the perfume counters.

As soon as you spray the perfume on your wrist you'll smell what is called the top note. An hour or two later the middle note will become apparent but it could take all day before you become aware of the true essence or base note. So, after trying two perfumes leave the shop and make a decision next day. You may have to visit a perfume counter several times before you discover the perfume for you!

MAKE AN IMPACT!

Keeping your favourite fragrance with you throughout the day should make you feel great – it's as much an extension of your personality as the clothes you wear, so use your perfume in the right way to ensure it **does** last.

Don't spray perfume over yourself as you dash out of the door as it'll evaporate in seconds. You should apply it to your pulse points as you dress – the warmth of your body will bring out the perfume's true notes. Your pulse points are located in the hollow of your throat, on your wrists, behind your knees and inside your elbows. The traditional idea of dabbing perfume behind your ears isn't necessarily right as your skin secretes slightly different oils in this area which might affect the perfume's fragrance.

If you can afford the original outlay you'll save in the end if you buy soap, bath oils and talc to match your perfume. Using all these products is called layering and you'll get a longer-lasting effect with less perfume.

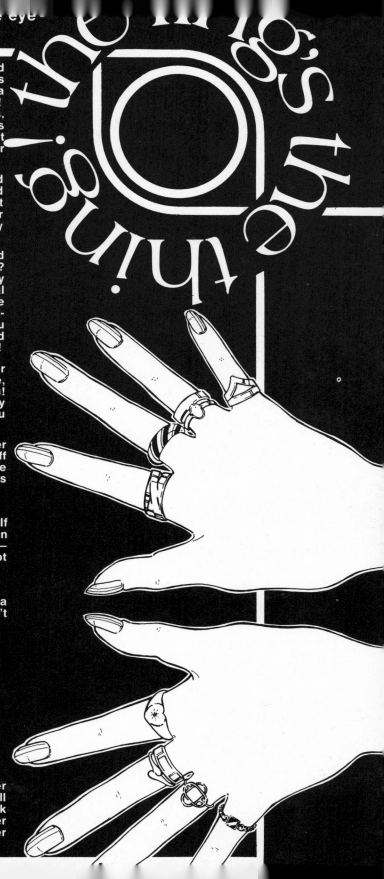

Rings have always been symbols of love, and giving one to someone you're fond of has always meant that you're not only making a present of a band of metal, but of your heart and affection, too!

There are lots of superstitions about rings, though, and if you check to see on which fingers you're wearing your rings, it'll tell you more about yourself than you'd imagined. Read on — our feature will ring the changes!

★ A SINGLE RING on any finger of either hand means that you're a pretty independent lady, and you don't need anyone to love and care for — at least, not yet! You've a touch of bossiness in your nature and a stubborn streak, with both feet firmly on the ground.

★ The THIRD FINGER of the left hand's reserved for your wedding ring — but d'you know why? Because it's said that there's a vein running directly from that finger to your heart! In most continental countries, though, wedding rings are worn on the third finger of the right hand. Wearing a ring alongside the third finger of your left hand means that you need to feel secure in your relationships — and that you're keeping your eyes peeled for Mr Right!

★ A ring worn on the SECOND FINGER of either hand means that you're the steady, cautious type, hardly likely to let your emotions run away with you! Rather clinging, you take your relationships very seriously and feel really hurt if someone's let you down. A bit of a softy, in fact!

★ D'you wear a ring on the FIRST FINGER of either hand? It's a sure sign that you're a bit of a show-off and know exactly what you want in life. You like to be seen and heard, too, and a persistent streak means that you'll probably *get* whatever you want!

Sweet Dreams!
Have you dreamed of any kind of ring recently? If you have, the chances are that there will be an engagement in the family before the year's out — and if the ring was a gold one, you're in for a lot of happiness during the next few years!

The Ring's The Thing!
To bring yourself an extra helping of luck, wear a ring with your special birthstone and things won't go far wrong!

ARIES — The diamond or bloodstone.
TAURUS — The opal or moonstone.
GEMINI — The sapphire or topaz.
CANCER — The moonstone or crystal.
LEO — The ruby or diamond.
VIRGO — The agate or crystal.
LIBRA — The pearl or emerald.
SCORPIO — The topaz or opal.
SAGITTARIUS — The amethyst or sapphire.
CAPRICORN — The turquoise or onyx.
AQUARIUS — The garnet or amethyst.
PISCES — The amethyst or pearl.

And the things that rings are made of? Well, a silver ring means luck with money . . . . an iron ring will bring good health . . . a gold ring signifies luck and happiness and . . . wait for it . . . a copper ring will stave off cramp! Rush out for your copper rings, folks!

THE CLUTCHES OF DARKNESS

I really am sorry I can't go to this party tonight, but I've got loads of studying to catch up on.

I'll go on my own then, Alan. I promised Joan I'd be there . . .

THINGS WERE GREAT TILL ALAN'S EXAMS STARTED. NOW I SEEM TO SPEND ALL MY TIME ALONE.

But at the party . . .

Who's that guy over there, Joan? I don't think I've seen him before.

You wouldn't have—he's just moved into the flat downstairs. His name's Michael.

He's great-looking—

Forget it! All he's done since he came in is stand over there. He doesn't seem interested in anything—or anybody.

47

But she didn't regret it . .

WE'VE ONLY BEEN TOGETHER A WEEK AND WE'RE ALREADY SO CLOSE . . .

But that night . . .

Uhh . . . go away . . . leave me alone . . .

It won't work, Michael. It never does. You won't have her . . . You cannot . . .

OH! WHAT AN ODD DREAM! AND WHO WAS THAT STRANGE GIRL?

Sue was still thinking about the dream the next morning.

What are you doing here, Alan?

I want to talk to you about this new guy of yours.

It's not really any of your business!

But Sue—no-one knows anything about him! He's a complete stranger who just...

He's not a stranger to me, Alan. You see—I love him.

But later . . .

Hello, Sue. Is there something wrong?

You can't! You know nothing about him! I don't trust him, Sue.

Leave me alone, Alan. Leave us both alone— Michael and me.

I just met Alan. I don't really like hurting him, Michael, that's all.

And what's more, I couldn't get to sleep last night because of a crazy dream about a girl who . . .

What girl? What sort of dream?

Later . . .

HE BEHAVED SO ODDLY WHEN I MENTIONED THAT DREAM—AS IF HE'D HEARD OF IT BEFORE . . .

And that night, the dream came again . . .

You won't get him, you know. He's mine—he'll always be mine. He'll never be free . . . Remember, Sue—he's mine—and will be forever.

Next morning Sue phoned Michael, and he came over straight away.

That strange girl—-she scared me, Michael—I don't know why.

Don't worry, Sue. I love you —I won't let anything hurt you.

I love you, too, Michael.

Do you really, Sue? Do you? You must tell me the truth . . .

I'd never lie about something like that.

I'm glad. Look—tonight I'll explain everything to you, I promise. At the little bridge outside town . . .

Later . . .

Alan! What are you doing here?

I had to see you—to try to reason with you. Please, can't we . . .

I'm sorry, Alan, but this is what I want. I love Michael—I know I do.

No, Sue! You can't love him! Maybe you'll change your mind when I tell you what I've found out about him—

Alan, just leave me alone! Michael's going to explain everything to me tonight. I'm meeting him at the little bridge outside town.

WHY WON'T ALAN LEAVE ME ALONE? I BET HE'S JUST JEALOUS.

When Sue met Michael . . .

I'm glad you came Sue. Come on—we must go to the bridge.

But why—?

Sue broke away from him then . . .

Michael, it—it's the girl from my dream. What's going on? I—I'm scared.

I thought you said you loved me! You said you loved me!

I—I know what I said. But Michael—that girl. Who is she?

Don't worry. We can fight her—and win!

Then, from the bridge, came a scream and the awful sound of twisting, crashing metal . . .

There's been a crash on the bridge! Someone may be hurt!

Sue! Come back! You must come back!

And, on the bridge . . .

Oh, no—it's that girl—and—Michael! Wh-what's going on here?

50

Sue could hardly believe what happened next . . .

He is destined to be by my side—he will never escape me!

Sue, you—you have to let me explain.

Oh, Michael—you're hurt!

She rushed forward.

I—I promised I'd explain—listen to me . . .

It began centuries ago, when a young boy fell in love with a beautiful girl, Lisa . . .

But he found that she was cruel and selfish and they parted. The boy met another girl, and they planned to wed.

But Lisa could not bear this, and she asked the village witchwoman to help . . .

Aye. I'll make sure your spirit and the lad's will be together for all time . . .

One day soon after, when the boy was riding, Lisa ran in front of his horse and made it rear.

The girl was kicked, the boy thrown. They both died . . .

And, just as the witchwoman promised, they were joined for all time. Their spirits can never rest but are destined to wander together for all eternity.

But—what have I to do with all this?

When a—a girl descendant of—of my true love is born, I am granted the right to come back as a mortal and try to break the spell. I can only escape my lonely wanderings if I take back to the spirit world a girl who I love truly and who loves me in return.

I was going to take you, Sue. I thought you loved me truly. But you couldn't have. You couldn't have . . .

You—you were going to take me . . .

Suddenly Michael was gone. Then . . .

You must come with me now. You will make me even stronger. You shall join the spirits of all the others he has tried to entice on to his side, and soon Michael will not be able to fight me.

N—no. Leave me—please . . .

Suddenly it was as if Michael was beside her again . . .

Sue! Think of the one person you truly love! Only he can save you from Lisa now . . .

ALAN! OH, ALAN—SAVE ME. PLEASE HELP ME!

You won't escape me, Sue . . .

Then—

A-Alan! Oh Alan, you're here! But how did you know?

You may have escaped me, but Michael won't, ever . . .

I—went to see Michael yesterday —he told me a weird story of spirits and spooks. He said only I could save you from . . . from him and Lisa . . .

He said something about re-enacting a death scene. I was worried, Sue. He seemed so strange and he seemed to believe that weird story. He almost had me believing it, which is why I came here tonight.

It—it was true, Alan. Everything he told you. I don't know how—or why—but tonight we became a part of something cold and dark and terrible . . .

It's over now, Sue—and it proved our love is strong again.

Yes—too strong to save poor Michael, but strong enough to save me from Lisa. Oh, Alan— I'm so glad it's over . . .

THE END

52

ARE YOU GAME FOR A PARTY?

It's the party season again and, just like it was when you were a kid, people still play party games. Only now, if you look closely, you'll notice that the games have changed just a bit. They may sound similar to the old familiar children's games, but there's a world of difference! So gen up on our guide to grown-up party games and make sure you're not caught with your tinsel in a twist this year!

MUSICAL CHASE

Chairs are placed around the room. Gorgeous Graham sits on one and Disgusting Dave on another. The aim of the game is to try to move as far away as possible from Dave's leers and B.O. and as near as possible to Graham's burning eyes and discreet after-shave. You can only move when the talking stops — so make sure you're miles away from Gossipy Gill or Gushing Greta. What's more, the music's blaring so loud that it's difficult to tell when the talking *has* stopped, and it's so dark it's easy to lose your sense of direction. But Graham's after-shave and Dave's B.O. should help you to get your bearings . . .

POSTMAN'S LOCK-OUT

In this variation on Postman's Knock, the crummiest boy at the party (usually a groper, an interloper or a no-hoper) is led astray by a brave volunteer (more than likely Geraldine the Queen's Guide). She dances cheek to cheek with him and when he starts to get fresh she whispers in his ear that it would be much more romantic and fun to smooch outside under the stars. But so's not to arouse suspicion, he's got to go outside first and she'll join him in a minute, when nobody's looking. So out creeps the creep, and once he's safely installed behind the rhododendrons, bingo! The door's locked and bolted, and the intrepid Geraldine is revived with a Coke and ice-cream and the heartfelt thanks of the entire company.

HUNT THE CONTACT LENS

This is a very fashionable game nowadays. It begins with an ear-splitting screech: "HEEEEELP! My lens!" Which brings the entire party to a halt. The girl (or boy) who's lost a lens stands stock-still with a hand clapped over one eye and the others have to crawl round on all fours on the carpet until the lens is found or the insurance comes through — whichever's quicker. Cigarette ends, ring-pulls from cans, old bus tickets and dead mice may also be found in dark corners, but unless the victim's prepared to shove it in her eye, it won't be counted as a genuine lens.

LUCKY DIP IN THE DARK

There are two versions of this game. First of all, you have to decide, in the pitch-black party "lighting," whether the guy who's asking you to dance is the dish of the evening or the Thing from the swamp. (You'll soon realise when you start dancing — if it's the Thing he won't be able to keep his tentacles to himself.)

The second version of Lucky Dip in the Dark takes place while you're enjoying a frenzied bop. The person who's "IT" sneaks away and goes through all the handbags, coats, etc., which are all piled up and unattended in the spare bedroom. Then he slips away into the night with his haul — which can be considerable. For the guy who's "IT" it can be a very Lucky Dip indeed.

SNIDE AND CHIC

The person who's "IT" goes out of the room. Instantly a deafening explosion of gossip breaks out. "Doesn't she look a mess in that awful dress, and her hair looks like an ostrich's nest, and what about those earrings, they look like something she got out of a cracker, and with legs like that she'd better keep out of the way of woodpeckers, etc., etc. . .". The winner is the one who manages to get the most snide comments in before the person who's "IT" comes back. Then the winner says to her, "Oh, Cheryl, we were just saying how *terrific* you look tonight. Where did you get those fantastic earrings?"

PASS THE BORING CREEP

There's always a boring creep at a party, and if you've failed to get rid of him with Postman's Lock-Out, your only chance is to play Pass the Boring Creep. The idea is to keep him moving from hand to hand so fast he won't have a chance to bore anyone to death. So if he comes your way, say, "Excuse me, Jim, but I must see to the sausage rolls. Have you met Helen?" Then you zoom off, and it's up to Helen to say, "Oh, sorry, Jim, but I promised my mum I'd ring her to say I'd arrived safely. Do you know Cheryl?" And then it's up to Cheryl.

Sometimes people playing Pass the Boring Creep get so desperate they shout, "HEEEEEELP! My lens!" and clap their hand over one eye, thus signalling the start of Hunt the Contact Lens instead. If really desperate, people have been known to shout, "HEEEEEELP! My lens!" even if they don't wear contact lenses. This makes Hunt the Contact Lens much more interesting.

ALL CHANGE!

A Jackie short story by Denise Leppard

My love life was turning into a game of musical chairs, what with all the swopping that was going on! Now there was only one option left, but it was the best of the lot!

AS Andrea and I set off to meet Dave and Simon for our usual Friday evening date, you'd be forgiven for thinking we didn't look too cheerful at the prospect. We weren't. Andrea was still having a fit of the sulks left over from our Wednesday date when by a show of hands we'd decided to forgo the Friday disco in favour of a film.

Andrea, who wanted to go dancing, was in a minority of one and had a row with her boyfriend Dave over him not siding with her. She'd also had a row with me because I hadn't wanted to go to the disco either, but when I showed her my feet, still bruised from the last time Simon trampled all over them, she had to admit I had a point.

"I'm sure Dave said he wanted to see the film just to annoy me," she said, still seething. "He knows I like that new group who're playing at the disco tonight."

"It would be worse if he agreed with every word you said, like Simon does with me," I told her. "It gets dead boring at times."

"Oh, Simon's *nice*," she said seriously. "You don't know how lucky you are, Judi."

"I suppose so," I answered dispiritedly. "But I sometimes wish we had a few ups and downs like you and Dave."

"Ups and downs! Ha!" She snorted. "He's just too bossy by half. Forever telling me to stop biting my nails or laughing too loud and showing him up. And look how he organises our dates — we always go where *he* says!"

"Well, Simon *never* has any good ideas," I pointed out morosely.

We contemplated the situation as we trudged down the road to the bus stop. We'd been going out with Dave and Simon for a couple of months now, and though it had been great to begin with, we were both beginning to have doubts. Once or twice I even wondered whether we'd each picked the wrong guy. I seemed to get on well with Dave, and Andrea thought Simon was the best thing since sliced bread.

Personally I thought anyone who reminded you of sliced bread was a big yawn.

We reached the bus stop and Simon gave me his slow smile. Dave pointedly looked at his watch and gave Andrea a scowl that matched hers.

"You're late," he said. "Another few minutes and we'd have missed the bus."

What Andrea replied was fortunately drowned in the gush of air brakes as the bus drew up. It couldn't have been very complimentary and the air was very frosty indeed as we got on. Things hadn't improved by the time we got off either.

"For Pete's sake, cheer up," Dave muttered to Andrea as we queued outside the cinema.

"How d'you expect me to look when I'm facing two hours of this boring film?" she spat back.

"Oh, I suppose you've thought of something fantastic that we could do instead?" he snapped.

"Yeah, like going to the disco," she said. "And seeing a few smiling faces for a change."

"Well, yours won't fit," he retorted. "Besides which, I think discos are *boring.*"

I could see World War Three breaking out before my very eyes, and also I felt a sneaking agreement with Dave.

"I suppose they are if we go all the time," I said, wriggling my bruised toes. "I think the film will make a nice change, actually."

Dave smiled at me, and Andrea glared. Faced with total opposition she might have grudgingly given in. However, Simon picked that moment to wake up from his customary trance.

"I don't mind going to the disco," he said equably.

"Well, I *do,*" I snapped.

"Right," Dave said, coming to an instant decision. "There's only one way to solve this. Simon takes Andrea to the disco and Judi and I'll go to the film. That way no-one's bored," he added with a final glare at Andrea.

"There you go — organising everyone again!" Andrea accused.

"Don't raise your voice, you're showing me up," Dave said tightly.

Hostilities were on the verge of erupting all over the pavement. Hastily I took Dave's arm.

"Look, if we're splitting up, we'd better go now," I said. "Let's meet up at the usual place afterwards for coffee."

"And we'll tell you what a good film you missed," Dave said, unable to resist the urge for a final crack.

"We'll see you later then," Andrea said with a glimmer of a smile I knew wouldn't be there after two hours of Simon thumping all over her feet.

ACTUALLY, to my surprise, the smile *was* still on her face when we met up at the coffee bar. She and Simon were laughing and joking when we arrived, though they fell silent and looked a bit guilty when we sat down. I was rather glad about that guilty look because I had one of my own. Dave had been holding my hand for the last half of the film and I'd quite enjoyed it. It completely made up for the embarrassing incidents in the first half when he'd told me to stop sniffing and suggested that I ate my popcorn in the interval as it was spoiling his concentration on the film.

"Enjoy the film?" Andrea asked me as we slid into our usual places.

"Er . . . yes, it was very good," I said.

"Did you enjoy the disco?" Dave asked, and she actually smiled at him.

"It was super," she said. "Wasn't it, Simon?"

54

"Yes, super," Simon agreed. "Sorry I trod on your foot, though."

"Oh, it was nothing, really," she told him sweetly, but I noticed she had her shoes off and was massaging her feet under the table.

By and large the evening finished much more satisfactorily than it had begun. Well, almost. I had to admit to a sneaking disappointment when we split up as usual and Simon walked me home. I wasn't exactly enthralled with the way he kept telling me what a nice time he'd had with Andrea at the disco and what a nice girl she was, either.

The next morning Andrea told me she'd had another row with Dave on the way home because he'd kept telling *her* what a nice time he'd had with me and what a nice girl I was.

"Oh?" I said with interest. "That was just what Simon kept saying about you."

"Really?" she said, perking up. "Strange that, because I got on with him quite well. I can't see how you find him so boring."

"Well, to be honest, I don't see why you complain about Dave so much," I told her. "He was quite good fun last night."

Andrea was eyeing me speculatively. "I wasn't going to tell you this," she went on slowly. "Because I didn't want to upset things between you and me, but . . . well, when Dave kept on about you last night I sort of told him that if you were as wonderful as that he ought to take you out instead of me. And he . . . well, he said he'd been thinking about it. In fact, he and Simon have talked about it, and Simon agreed."

"He would," I said thoughtfully, then stopped in my tracks. "Do you want to swap?" I asked her.

"I wouldn't mind," she told me cautiously. "I don't think things are going to improve between Dave and me. And quite honestly, I've been wondering for some time whether we'd paired up with the wrong guys . . ."

So we swapped.

On Saturday night, at Dave's suggestion, we had a conference and discussed the situation, and after an initial bout of giggling firmly suppressed by Dave, Andrea went and sat next to Simon, and Dave took my hand in a very proprietorial manner. Later we went down to the disco and it was wonderful not to have my toes trodden on once.

"We should have thought of this earlier," I said to Andrea on the way to school on Monday.

"Mm, I haven't enjoyed myself so much for ages," she agreed. "It's so relaxing being with Simon after having Dave boss me around for so long."

I didn't like to tell her that was how I'd felt when I first went out with Simon. "I like being with Dave," I said. "He's got a mind of his own and doesn't mind speaking up for himself. Look how he told me he didn't like my new lipstick. Some boys wouldn't bother. And I'm glad he told me he thought my dress was too short."

Andrea gave me a knowing look, but I smiled cheerfully. After all, we both knew we'd got the right partners now.

I SUPPOSE we spent about two weeks telling each other how pleasant it was and enthusing over how different Simon/Dave was and what a great time we were having. Only, I was privately beginning to think it wasn't that great after all. I was discovering disadvantages in having a self-opinionated boyfriend. Like his constant nagging about my supposed faults, and the way he thought nothing about holding public arguments over them.

And I noticed Andrea was doing a lot more yawning these days when we were out. Once when we were all listening to records round at her house one evening she actually dropped right off to sleep and it was ages before anyone noticed.

Dave and I had three private tussles and two public ones over me wiping my nose on my finger, which I don't — it's a nervous habit and it only looks like I do — before he told me off for fidgeting with my hair, taking deep breaths in the cinema which disturbed his concentration and talking with my mouth full, after which I began to go off him.

I also noticed that he generally took it on himself to decide where we were going without consulting anyone. Simon always agreed with him, and Andrea, who'd lost her energy due to her new relaxed attitude towards life, simply tagged along yawning, willing to go anywhere so long as it wasn't the disco on account of the state of her trampled feet.

The pair of us were early at the bus stop for our usual Friday date, due to me not wanting to risk another argument with Dave over being late. Andrea looked as unexcited as I did at the prospect of seeing yet another film chosen by Dave, with the usual coffee and the usual walk home followed by the usual arrangements for Saturday.

"There's a new youth club opening at the town hall tonight," Andrea said listlessly. "They've got a group and a live D.J. and it looks like being fun."

"Yeah, I read it in the local paper," I added. "Lots of the girls at school are going. Pity we're going to see this film. I'd like to have gone to the town hall."

She sighed. "But Dave doesn't like clubs, does he?"

"There's not a lot he does like," I said mournfully. "Except his own way. I suppose we'll have to sit through this boring old film with Dave telling me not to fidget and stop scratching or something."

"I can always go to sleep," she said with a another sigh. "Simon wouldn't notice anyway."

"I told you what he was like," I pointed out.

"And I warned you about Dave. I was right, wasn't I?"

I looked at her hopefully. "You don't want him back, do you?"

"Why?" she hedged. "Do you want to have Simon back?"

"No, thank you," I burst out with such a look of horror that she laughed. "In fact, I don't want either of them," I added. "I reckon you and I would have more fun on our own."

"I've been thinking that for ages," she agreed, looking more alive than she had for weeks. "We used to go out with the girls and go to all sorts of places and have *fun*, or even just stay in and listen to records if we felt like it. These two have got to be a real drag."

We looked along the road where Dave and Simon were just turning the corner. Dave was pulling up his sleeve to look at his watch and frowning.

"Pity we couldn't ditch them now," I said. "We could go to that new club. I bet we'd have a fantastic time. Meet some new blokes."

"We've got to get rid of the old ones first," Andrea whispered, the light of dread all over her face. "How do we do it? What do we say?"

"It's easy," I told her with a grin, linking my arm with hers as we waited for Dave and Simon to reach us. "One little word that we should have said weeks ago — GOODBYE!"

CHRISTMAS SHOPPING CAN BE FUN!
(but it never is)

Just think—soon you, too, can join the pushing, shoving throngs and stampede your way towards shop counters, eager to hand over your piggy bank full of 20p pieces.

But before you buy your presents, you have to face the dreaded Shop Assistant—and some of them can be very dreadful indeed. We've been having a fun look at some of the types you're likely to come across and given you some ideas on how to deal with them . . .

THE COSMETIC CONSULTANT

This one must be the most dreaded of all. There she stands behind the cosmetic and perfume counter, immaculately made-up, making you feel like an untidy worm who's just crawled out from under the nearest stone. You take a gulp and move in nervously as the first waft of expensive perfume hits you and the eyelashes like spiky tarantulas swivel in your direction, obviously wondering what a grotty little specimen like you could possibly want from someone like *her*.

DON'T

. . . ask for something "smelly."

. . . say, "Five pounds for *those?*" when she shows you three bath cubes.

. . . let her see you're terrified of her.

DO

. . . tell her there seems little choice compared to the shops in Paris.

. . . describe perfumes as "too floral / unsubtle / woody / heady" rather than "too expensive."

THE BOOK SHOP BUFFOON

Your dad wants a gardening book, so to keep him happy, you decide to brave the terrors of the book

shop. And terrifying it is, too, since every book shop seems to have its resident spotty, creepy young assistant who thinks he's so attractive you'll fall into his arms at the first sight of his shiny suit and greasy tie. The fact that you'd rather fall over a cliff than into his arms never enters his dandruffed head.

As you stand there trying to decide between "Mow Your Own Lawn" and "Rose Manure For Fun," one of these specimens will appear at your elbow.

DON'T

. . . smile at him. You don't want to encourage the poor soul.

. . . ask his advice about gardening books. He won't have a clue since all he ever reads are the back of Cornflake packets and the instructions for applying his acne cream.

DO

. . . arrange to meet him on his half day. Then you can stand him up, nip back to the shop and browse in peace.

. . . say you'll make a point of telling his boss how helpful

he's been. This'll scare the spots off him since he's actually the store room shelf cleaner and shouldn't even be in the shop in the first place.

THE ANCIENT IRONMONGER

Your boyfriend wants a set of flange nuts for Christmas. You haven't a clue what these are but you do know you have to enter the unknown territory of the ironmonger's to buy them. Once you get over your embarrassment at being the only female in the shop, you approach the counter where the only assistant, an ancient person in an old brown overall with pencils and screwdrivers behind his ears, asks you what you want.

DON'T

. . . mumble. Ancient Ironmongers tend to be deaf (because of all the screwdrivers and pencils in their ears).

. . . try to pretend you know what you're talking about. If you do, he'll only ask you if you want the 6 in. flange nuts with grockle spindles or the 4 in. ones with screwhead

adaptors. And then what will you say?

DO

. . . just give your boyfriend the money and tell him to buy his own flange nuts. It may not seem very romantic, but then neither is a boyfriend who wants flange nuts for Christmas.

THE SHOE SHOP GOSSIPS

Now there's only the pink fluffy slippers to buy for your gran. Easy, you think. Just walk into the shoe shop, pick up the slippers and hand them to the assistant. But—now you come up against the Gossip. You won't normally find a Gossip on her own. There's generally two of them and they spend their days standing behind shop counters engrossed in interesting conversations about things like Mrs Edwards' varicose veins.

DON'T

. . . cough in an attention seeking fashion. If you do that, they'll ignore you even more.

. . . march over and stand and stare at them. They'll only move further off down the counter and continue their conversation.

. . . decide just to wait until they've finished. They won't finish their little chat until 5.30 when they'll tell you you're too late to buy anything because the shop's just closing.

DO

. . . say, in a bored sort of way, "Mrs Edwards? That wasn't varicose veins she had. My mum's a nurse and she should know." This is guaranteed to get their attention.

. . . take the size 4 £85 boots off the stand and try to cram your size 7's into them. One of the Gossips will be right behind you to "help." That's when you produce your gran's fluffy slippers.

How To Cope When He Says Goodbye

IT'S finally happened. He's told you he doesn't want to see you any more. Your whole world's collapsed and you can't imagine how you're going to get through life without him. But you can — and you will. What's more, you can almost chart your progress through a break-up. Your timing and your speed will depend on you as an individual, but you can be sure you'll go through all the normal stages of crying over him, missing him, remembering all the good times and, unbelievable as it seems at the moment, getting over him.

The first thing you'll do is cry for him

So go ahead and cry. Lock your bedroom door and cry till you want to. Stare at his picture. Torture yourself with the thought that you'll never see him again. Imagine him kissing his new girl. And cry some more.

Then you'll think it was all your fault

This is when that awful phrase, "*If only*" creeps into your thoughts. You think, "*If only I'd been more understanding about that other girl,*" or, "*If only I'd been more interested in snooker,*" or you could even think, if you've got it badly enough, "*If only I was prettier he wouldn't have chucked me.*" Well — forget it!

Chuck out all the if-onlys and might-have-beens and start to shift the blame a little. Instead of feeling it's all your fault, think about how awful **he** was. Think about how creepy he was to go out with that other girl; think about how selfish he was to expect you to put up with him playing snooker five nights a week; think about how you're actually **too** pretty for a toad like him.

Think anything you like as long as you start to feel good and **angry** with him.

Then it's time to face the truth

Now you finally admit it's over. You stop hoping, stop waiting for the phone to ring and stop dreaming about the big reunion scene.

Now's the time to keep your tears for when you're alone. Now's the time to resist the temptation to blurt everything out to anyone who'll listen.

And while you're facing the truth, ring all your mutual friends and tell them you've split. It's easier to get this out of the way quickly and you'll be relieved once everyone knows.

You'll find that quite a few mutual friends will prove to be less mutual, so be prepared for this.

Be prepared, too, for everyone to ask, "Where's Bert/Steve/Harry?" as if you were permanently glued together — which you were, of course.

Trouble is, you've been two

for so long, you've forgotten how to be alone. But it can be fun!

Now's the time to go crazy and be adventurous. Make yourself over, take up new interests. Don't play safe with flower-pressing or cookery classes — try tap-dancing, self-defence classes or a drama group.

Now's the time to face up to yourself

Use the break-up positively. Take decisions you've always put off and do things you've always wanted to do. If you've always wanted to go Youth Hostelling, or take dance classes, or try your hand at motor cycle maintenance but always put it off because of him, now's the time to strike out.

You've no-one else to think about now, so you can be as selfish and independent as you like.

You're almost cured now

It won't all be plain sailing, of course. Just when you think you're beginning to get over him, some little incident will set you off again. This is when you start to think you'd give it all up, if only

you could have those times back.

But that feeling doesn't last long and you're now halfway towards being able to remember the special things about your relationship without pain. Now, too, you're well on the way to remembering what you loved about him without necessarily wanting him back.

Now you can start again

Now you're ready to face the world again. Your cousin's twenty-first party may not sound like fun — but go anyway. You'll be meeting people, and that's what counts.

Try not to compare new experiences with the way things used to be. What you had was very special — and that kind of relationship doesn't happen every day, or with every boy.

Complete recovery — The test

You see him again — and everything you've worked for hangs in the balance. Resist the temptation to ignore him.

Face him. Smile at him. The sheer satisfaction of knowing you look good, knowing you've survived,

will be worth the willpower it takes to smile and chat to him for a minute or two.

Chances are you'll think he's changed and you may wonder how you could have spent so much time and trouble getting over someone who's so — well — *ordinary*.

Getting over a break up, starting all over again, isn't a case of slamming a door on one part of your life and opening a new one. It's much slower than that and a much more complicated process. It's a bit like wandering along corridors when you're not too sure of the way.

The most important factor in your recovery is time. Gradually, instead of only acting as if you're over the heartbreak, you'll find it's true.

You'll admit you wouldn't have missed out on the relationship, even though it made you more miserable than you've ever been. You've been in love — and out of love. It's a crazy merry-go-round and you're getting ready to jump on all over again . . .

SUPERSTITIOUS

Are you ever seen in red and green,
Eating an apple every day?
Does the full moon at night give you a fright,
Has a black cat come your way?
Does a shattered mirror give you a quiver,
Will you cross your fingers and bow?
Go on – be plucky and see if you're lucky
– Try our quiz right now!

1. You'll have heard that an apple a day keeps the doctor away — but what about strawberries? Do they have any magical qualities?
  a. Yes, they bring you out in an itchy rash.
  b. Yes, they keep your teeth lovely and clean.
  c. Yes — they cost a lot of money and keep you awake at night with stomach pains.

2. If you spotted two crossed knives on the kitchen worktop just before you went out to meet your new fella, would you:
  c. shove them in a drawer — you don't need bad luck,
  a. assume that your mum's used them to chop up your salad — and think nothing more of

  b. panic — that means you're going to quarrel — or worse still, he won't turn up at all?

3. You've chosen a leather purse to give your mate for her birthday. Before you wrap it, do you:
  b. slip a coin inside it,
  a. take the price tag off,
  c. write "Happy Birthday" on a small card and pop it inside?

4. You bash your mascara brush against the mirror and it smashes, silly! Do you:
  a. carry on getting ready,
  c. sink into a deep depression — how are you going to cope with seven years' bad luck,
  b. make yourself even later by

burying them in the back garden?

5. You're chatting away to a guy at a party, when you accidentally drop one of your gloves. Do you:
  c. whistle conspicuously and hover around till someone picks it up for you,
  a. quickly snatch it up off the floor — crossing your fingers and hoping that nothing terrible will happen to you,
  b. loiter around till someone picks it up, but don't say thanks when they hand it to you?

6. You've sneaked down to the kitchen in the middle of the night for a secret snack. You're chomping your way through the chicken when — gasp! — you spot a cut onion on the table. Do you:
  b. scream — it's a dreadful omen and something awful's going to happen,
  c. feel rather worried — you'll probably have a nightmare when you go back to bed,

MINDS!

bracelet 'cos you've heard that magpies nick things,

c. carry on walking — but keep your eyes peeled, in case you can spot its mate?

your mum to leave things lying about?

a. Sunday.

7. Which day of the week would you most like to have been born on?
c. Monday.
b. Friday.

8. You're out for a nice, healthy stroll in the country, when you spot a magpie on a fence. Do you:
b. quake with fear and cross your fingers till you see another one,
a. keep tight hold of your gold

9. You've been invited round to your fella's to meet his folks. You're all set to impress them when his mum dishes out the tea. Suddenly, someone drops a fork, so do you:
c. fling your plate over your shoulder,
a. throw a handful of salt over your shoulder,
b. feel slightly suspicious and ask your fella if he's expecting another visitor?

So, do superstitions drive *you* scatty — or d'you cringe with fear if someone so much as plonks their shoes on the table or peers at the new moon through a window? Take a peek at the real meanings of the superstitions — and tot up your score — mostly a's, b's or c's. All will be revealed!

SUPERSTITIONS RUN-DOWN!

1. A strawberry a day *could* be rather pricey and in vast quantities they may even upset your tum — but fresh strawberries are much more likely to keep your pearlies lovely and clean, 'cos they're great at removing tartar!
2. Crossed sword blades were always the starting point for a duel, so crossed knives mean that there's an argument brewing!
3. If you pop a coin into a purse before giving it away, it means that the purse will never be empty.
4. When you smash a mirror, the seven years of bad luck refer to the seven years it takes the body's cells to regenerate themselves! You can avoid bad luck, though, by burying the pieces or washing them in a running stream.
5. In medieval times, throwing down a glove was the challenge to a fight — so it's bad luck to pick up your own dropped glove. It's supposed to be unlucky to thank whoever picks it up for you, too — but we reckon that wouldn't make you too popular!
6. A cut onion's really unlucky — but for a practical reason. Onion flesh attracts all kinds of bacteria which could make you ill — so in this case, it makes sense to be superstitious!
7. Monday's child is fair of face. Friday's child is loving and giving. Sunday's child is fair, wise, good and gay. Take your pick!
8. Spotting a single magpie will bring sorrow, unless you cross your fingers, spit or bow to it!
9. A dropped fork means an unexpected male visitor — and if there's food on the table, it means he's going to turn up hungry!

CONCLUSIONS

Mostly a's
Practical and down-to-earth, hardly anything upsets you — least of all a few silly superstitions! On the surface, you seem to be lacking in imagination and take everything at face value. You've no time for old wives' tales — and as you're rather afraid of people laughing at you, you keep your emotions under control and look at everything in a logical way. Occasionally, though, you can be spotted avoiding ladders and crossing your fingers — not that you'd ever admit it, of course!

Mostly b's
You're the sort of person who won't travel on Friday the 13th — or look at a new moon through glass! Believing totally in all kinds of superstitions, proverbs and legends, you're convinced that there must be something in them — and walk around with your fingers crossed, just in case. You're a dreamer, not a doer, and constantly let your imagination run away with you — which lands you in trouble from time to time, as you're the most impractical among us! As you're the proverb says, look before you leap — and keep your wits about you once in a while!

Mostly c's
Lucky you — you've a fortunate streak that'll make sure that you always land on your feet! You're practical and level-headed — and a strong believer in good and bad luck, although an unlucky omen or bad sign won't send you into a state of panic. You're intelligent and great fun to have around — and although you're often labelled as the sensible one, you've a zany sense of humour, too. Yes, superstitions are important to you, and you'd probably avoid walking under a ladder. Not if it meant having to walk out into a busy street, though!

Mari Wilson:

"Mine was a black doll that I was given when I was three years old. You could style her hair in all different ways. Some friends gave it to me and I've kept it ever since. It's still in my room and I'll never get rid of it because it means so much to me. Absolutely no-one is allowed to touch it!"

It's A Christmas (W)rap!

Find out about these pop stars' favourite Christmas pressies!

Kevin Rowland, Dexy's:

"My favourite Christmas present is everything and anything — I just love receiving gifts! I never keep the gorgeous wrapping paper all neat and tidy — it always gets all ripped to shreds as I frantically look to see what goodies I've got!"

Michael Mullins, Modern Romance:

"My most unforgettable Christmas present was my first record-player. It was great to be able to escape to your room and listen to your favourite records. And ever since that first record-player I've been hooked on pop music."

Nick Heyward:

"When I was at school, my favourite subject was art and I did quite well at it. All of my spare time was spent drawing, but I always wanted a really good art set of my own with expensive paints and brushes. Then at Christmas when I was about fourteen years old, there it was. I really treasured it!"

Chris Foreman, Madness:

"I think it would probably have been the first proper bicycle I had. I loved cycling, and still do, but nothing can beat that first bike. I used to spend hours cleaning it even if it didn't need it!"

Phil Oakey, The Human League:

"My best pressie was from my record company, Virgin. They gave me a motorbike to zoom around on.

"It was a really nice gesture which I really appreciated and kept me very enthusiastic about being involved in the music business."

Kate Garner, Haysi Fantayzee:

"It's difficult trying to think which was the best, but it would probably be a pair of roller-skates that I had when I was quite young. I drove everyone mad on them, racing around the house. I can remember falling over quite a bit too, but eventually I was an expert. My ambition was always to go roller-racing!"

Jim Kerr, Simple Minds:

"Books were always one of my favourite presents, particularly if they had anything to do with travel and adventure. I guess the best of the batch that really kept me going for ages was a large atlas which I spent ages looking at and planning imaginary journeys. Also a copy of 'Robinson Crusoe.'"

DON'T LOOK NOW – IT'S SUPERYAWN!

You know the feeling — you're halfway through a detailed description of Granny's birthday party when suddenly you notice your mate's glazed expression as her eyelids begin to droop. In other words, she's BORED — and you're BORING! So how d'you beat the boring blues? Read on, discover your own brand of bore, and you'll never have to face another yawn!

CONDITION: THE GRUMBLE-BORE
REMEDY:

Only the boring are bored, as the saying goes, and it's true, too! It stands to reason that those among us who slither out of bed amid grumbles and groans, slouch to school with a face of thunder and fester the evening away in front of the telly aren't the most dynamic or exciting of people. If life bores you, it's impossible to summon up the slightest scrap of enthusiasm for any goings-on, and with a sullen expression, you'll spend life with a constant chip on your shoulder. In other words, you're a Grumble-Bore — of the very worst kind!

Think about it, and if you suspect you're boring, analyse your attitude to life in general. There's nothing more irritating than having a Grumble-Bore around — someone who's totally fed-up and lives under a huge, grey cloud, constantly reminding everyone of the fact. The first step in breaking out of the super-yawn trap is to banish your boredom, so work up a little more enthusiasm for life — whether it's the countryside you love or a gorgeous sunrise — and you'll be a whole lot more fun to have around!

CONDITION: THE SELF-BORE
REMEDY:

We're all guilty of looking after number one, flattering ourselves and guarding our own interests. It's when this feeling of self-importance gets out of hand that you're well on the way to becoming a self-bore! You'll have heard people rambling on about their talents and achievements — boring all in sight — and the tragedy is that Self-Bores just don't seem to notice their audience of stifled yawns. Are you a Self-Bore? If you suspect that, yes, you do ramble on about number one, take stock of yourself and resolve to keep your tongue under control in future.

Self-Bores, surprisingly, aren't as confident as they may seem. In fact, as well as trying to convince everyone in sight that they're amazingly talented and interesting, they're trying just as hard to prove to *themselves* that they're worthwhile. Perhaps you've admitted that you do go on rather a lot and you've realised that although people are interested in your new fella — and are dying to hear about your first date — they only want to hear about the man of your dreams once. By the third telling, the tale's lost its attraction — so instead of boosting your ego and boring all around you, show an interest in your friends. Ask questions, be willing to listen as well as chatter, and when you hear yourself begin, "You know what I did at the weekend . . .", — bite your

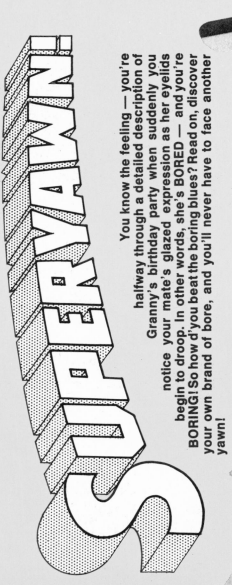

62

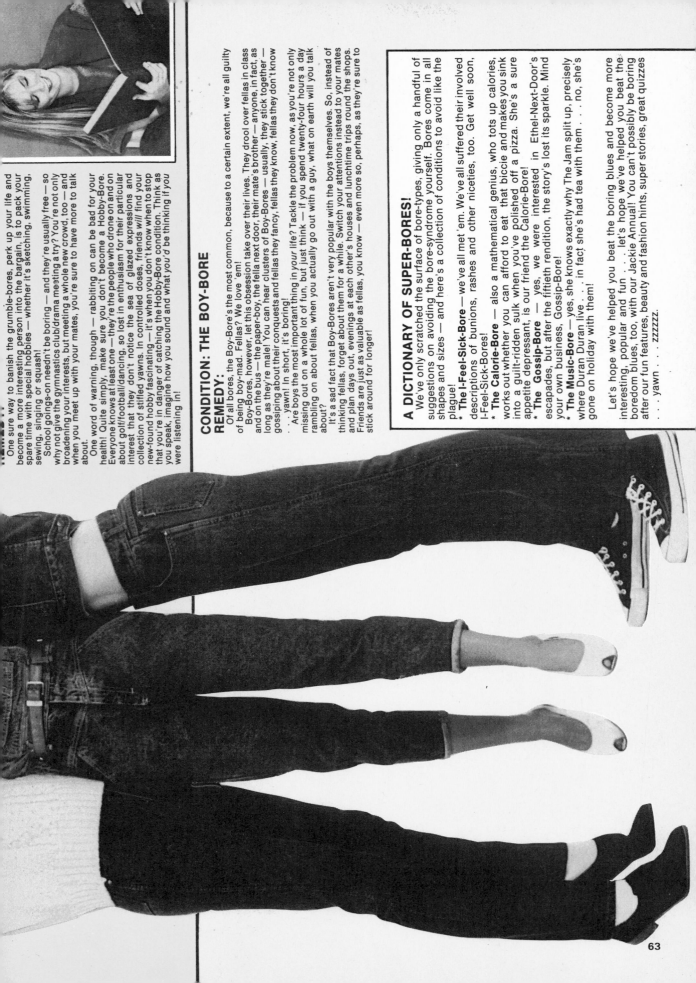

One sure way to banish the grumble-bores, perk up your life and become a more interesting person into the bargain, is to pack your spare time with special hobbies — whether it's sketching, swimming, sewing, singing or squash!

School goings-on needn't be boring — and they're usually free — so why not give the gymnastics club/drama meeting a try? You're not only broadening your interests, but meeting a whole new crowd, too — and when you meet up with your mates, you're sure to have more to talk about.

One word of warning, though — rabbiting on can be bad for your health! Quite simply, make sure you don't become a Hobby-Bore. Everyone knows at least one — they're the people who drone on and on about golf/football/dancing, so lost in enthusiasm for their particular interest that they don't notice the sea of glazed expressions and collection of stifled yawns. In controlled doses, friends *will* find your new-found hobby fascinating — it's when you don't know when to stop that you're in danger of catching the Hobby-Bore condition. Think as you speak, imagine how you sound and what *you'd* be thinking if you were listening in!

CONDITION: THE BOY-BORE REMEDY:

Of all bores, the Boy-Bore's the most common, because to a certain extent, we're all guilty of being boy-mad. Fellas? We love 'em!

Boy-Bores, however, let this obsession take over their lives. They drool over fellas in class and on the bus — the paper-boy, the fella next door, their mate's brother — anyone, in fact, as long as they're male! You can hear clusters of Boy-Bores — usually, they stick together — gossiping about their conquests and fellas they fancy, fellas they know, fellas they don't know . . . yawn! In short, it's boring!

Are boys the most important thing in *your* life? Tackle the problem now, as you're not only missing out on a whole lot of fun, but just think — if you spend twenty-four hours a day rambling on about fellas, when you actually go out with a guy, what on earth will you talk about?

It's a sad fact that Boy-Bores aren't very popular with the boys themselves. So, instead of thinking fellas, forget about them for a while. Switch your attentions instead to your mates and plan days out, evenings at each other's houses and lunchtime trips round the shops. Friends are just as valuable as fellas, you know — even more so, perhaps, as they're sure to stick around for longer!

A DICTIONARY OF SUPER-BORES!

We've only scratched the surface of bore-types, giving only a handful of suggestions on avoiding the bore-syndrome yourself. Bores come in all shapes and sizes — and here's a collection of conditions to avoid like the plague!

* **The I-Feel-Sick-Bore** — we've all met 'em. We've all suffered their involved descriptions of bunions, rashes and other niceties, too. Get well soon, I-Feel-Sick-Bores!

* **The Calorie-Bore** — also a mathematical genius, who tots up calories, works out whether you can afford to eat that biccie and makes you sink into a guilt-ridden sulk when you've polished off a pizza. She's a sure appetite depressant, is our friend the Calorie-Bore!

* **The Gossip-Bore** — yes, we were interested in Ethel-Next-Door's escapades, but after the fiftieth rendition, the story's lost its sparkle. Mind your own business, Gossip-Bore!

* **The Music-Bore** — yes, she knows exactly why The Jam split up, precisely where Duran Duran live . . . in fact she's had tea with them . . . no, she's gone on holiday with them!

Let's hope we've helped you beat the boring blues and become more interesting, popular and fun . . . let's hope we've helped you beat the boredom blues, too, with our Jackie Annual! You can't possibly be boring after our fun features, beauty and fashion hints, super stories, great quizzes . . . yawn . . . zzzzzz.

FOOTPRINTS IN THE SNOW

I knew about the other girl almost before you did, Sean — but I deliberately shut out the truth . . .

I'M sorry, Jen," Sean said. "I really am. It just happened. You know how it is."

"Yes," I said. But I didn't know.

I kept my back turned towards him, staring out of the window at the falling snow. It reminded me of how we met . . .

Last January — huge flakes of snow were falling when I hurried home from the tech, and by the time I'd had tea, it was sparkling in the light from the street lamp outside the window. Mum was washing up in the kitchen, bemoaning the fact that my little brother, Timmy, wasn't home from the Cubs, and she knew just where he'd be — up at the common playing snowballs and forgetting all about the time. Finally, she asked me if I'd go and fetch him, and I didn't mind — I was glad to escape from the tedium of shorthand homework and typing manuals.

Seven or eight small boys were circling an enormous snowman. One of them had perched a cap on the snowman's head — it turned out to be Timmy's.

They all gave a warning yell when they saw me, and Timmy tried to run, but I caught hold of him and demanded to know who'd pinched his cap. A little red-haired lad popped up cheekily beside us and admitted it — and at that moment, someone came up behind him and grabbed his arm.

"Sorry about this," the newcomer said. We stood facing each other in the snow. "My brother," he went on.

"Mine, too," I replied, indicating Timmy.

Sean retrieved the cap and I rammed it on Timmy's curly mop, while red-haired Brendan stood close by, grinning.

I smiled back at him. It was the least I could do — after all, if it hadn't been for both those little horrors, I'd never have met Sean . . .

We spent a lot of time together from then on, Sean and I. One wintry night we'd been out walking in the snow and, as we looked back, I saw two clear sets of footprints outlined behind us. Sean's and mine.

"Like an omen, that," he'd laughed. "Just the two of us, walking side by side."

"I had to tell you," he said now, crossing to the window and staring out. "It was snowing when we met," he said suddenly, surprised. "Do you remember?"

I nodded, not trusting myself to speak. I remember everything — the

snow melting, the sun shining weakly — everything.

THOSE long sunny days on the beach, where we swam from morning till night, then lay stretched out on the warm sand, eyes closed, hands touching. We knew it was for ever, you and I, Jen and Sean, partners . . .

Summer turned into a lazy, russet autumn, slipped almost imperceptibly into winter. And the parties began — your birthday, my birthday, Simon's sixteenth, Merrilyn's coming-of-age.

I knew before you really knew yourself, Sean. I saw you look at her, the slim, fair-haired girl who came on her own and stood by the door, smiling brightly, so desperately. I saw you look at her, stop in mid sentence. And then turn back to me with the eyes of a stranger. I knew then — I knew and ignored.

I didn't want to believe it. You seemed the same, afterwards. You tried to be, anyway — you took me home, made our usual date and cancelled it two days later, saying you had too much work . . .

"I wish you'd say something." Sean pressed a hand to the window-pane. The snow had stopped.

Dilys had told me, at last — had made me listen. She'd seen you, you and the fair-haired girl at the Christmas disco, the one I hadn't been able to go to.

But I still wouldn't listen. I still held on — through the rest of December and January, when you must have been torn — torn between the two of us. She and I.

And now?

"There isn't anything to say, Sean." I walked away from the window, went to the door, opened it. "Except goodbye."

You waited a moment, staring at me, wanting to say something more, not knowing what. Then you turned and walked out of the house.

I heard the click of the gate, and crossed on stiff legs back to the window. There, in the snow, lay a single set of footprints. Even as I stared through rapidly-filling eyes, the flakes began to fall again, covering completely the dark indentations, losing them for ever.

It was almost as if you had never existed. As if all my love had lived only in my imagination. And I wish it had. Because it would be so much easier to bear than this stark, cold, empty reality . . .

MADGE and BERYL

I'VE WRITTEN A TV SOAP OPERA — WOULD YOU HELP ME TO TEST IT, MADGE?

IT'S ABOUT TWO SISTERS — I'M RAPUNZEL AND YOU'RE VERA.

I'M EXOTIC, PRETTY AND ADMIRED BY ALL.

YOU'RE PLAIN, DRAB AND NOBODY LIKES YOU.

I HAVE A GLAMOROUS JOB AS A FASHION DESIGNER.

YOU WORK AT THE BACK OF A DRYCLEANER'S SEWING ON MISSING BUTTONS.

JUST A MINUTE, BERYL... I THINK I'M MORE LIKE RAPUNZEL.

CAN WE SWITCH PARTS?

ONE DAY WHEN RAPUNZEL GOES TO WORK, THE STUDIO HAS BURNT DOWN AND, PENNILESS, SHE LEAVES THE COUNTRY.

MEANWHILE VERA FINDS A MILLION POUND NOTE IN A JACKET SHE'S REPAIRING.

SHE SENDS IT TO THE OWNER OF THE JACKET WHO IS NONE OTHER THAN...

RICK SPENDMONEY III WHO, WHEN HE MEETS VERA...

..ER, I THINK VERA IS MORE LIKE ME..

..WHO, WHEN HE MEETS VERA IS MOST DISAPPOINTED AS SHE'S VERY BORING.

MEANWHILE RAPUNZEL RETURNS FROM ABROAD — NOW THE RICH OWNER OF A DESIGNER JEANS FIRM.

RAPUNZEL SNATCH!

RICK SPENDMONEY III HAS SECOND THOUGHTS AND PHONES VERA....

..THAT'S THE END OF THE FIRST EPISODE!

ER.. I THINK IT WOULD WORK BETTER IF THE SISTERS WERE TWINS — AND I PLAY THEM BOTH!

YOU CAN ALWAYS RELY ON ME TO GIVE A COMPLETELY UNBIASED OPINION, BERYL.

THANKS MADGE!

65

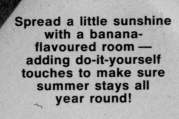

Spread a little sunshine with a banana-flavoured room — adding do-it-yourself touches to make sure summer stays all year round!

GONE BANANAS!

What better time than now to revamp your surroundings and let a little sunshine into your room? Giving your bedroom an updated touch needn't cost a fortune — just a little time, a collection of bright ideas and lots of imagination! Before you dash to the do-it-yourself shop, though, remember a few points and you won't go far wrong — the rest is up to you!

*Remember that you'll have to live with your room, and although black and blue stripes with a candy-pink ceiling may drive you into ecstacies for a day or two, they'll be driving you up the black-and-blue-striped wall after a fortnight.

*Don't leap into your room-revamping campaign without first thinking of a general style and colour scheme, or you'll end up with a bitty bedroom focussing on nothing in particular. We chose a fantastically-bright banana yellow, but soothing green, cool blue or hot red may be more in your line.

*Don't forget that pale colours make a room appear larger — and white comes tops when you're looking for cool, crisp space. If your room's short of windows and doesn't receive an awful lot of sun, opt for pastel shades and little clutter.

*Think, too, about your room's function. Sounds obvious? Well, say your room's the meeting place for your crowd of mates. Spick and span, sleek surroundings won't stay particularly spick and span after *that* lot have trailed in, will they? — so throw around a pile of scatter cushions and rugs and concentrate on a feeling of informal com-

fort. If you're a telly freak, make room for a comfy chair, or for your trays of make-up if you're our Beauty Ed's greatest rival. Make the room fit *you* — not the other way round!

Wonderful Windows!

The light source of a room's vital, so it stands to reason that windows play a pretty important part in your room, too! Heavy, dark curtains hardly let the sun stream through, though, so keep your eyes peeled for cheap fabric in a sunny shade. For a light, cool look, why not invest in a bright roller blind — venetian blinds may sound fuddy-duddy but they come in great primary shades now — so shop around!

Try painting your own, simple design on a roller blind with fabric paints from Dylon — they're available from most craft shops and department stores, costing around 80p. Paint random splashes, a bright beach scene or Chinese floral design — keep it simple, though!

Work It Out!

D'you read, write letters or tackle those maths problems in your room? Keep a workspace clear with stocks of pens at hand, neatly stored in matching pots. Cover empty cocoa tins and a chocolate box with wrapping paper, and keep your eyes peeled for bits 'n' pieces in your chosen shade. Wire baskets used to hold office paperwork make an ideal filing system — they

66

stack, too, so build 'em up high-rise. Check out Habitat stores for kitchen wall grids — those odds and ends will never get lost again! — and remember that wire vegetable racks hold all those papers, letters and old Jackies.

Keep your eyes open even in the most unlikely places — you may find the ideal container for your make-up in a do-it-yourself shop labelled as a toolbox, or a cake tin to hold all those pens. All it takes is a little imagination!

Plump For Pillows!

Add huge floor-cushions for instant comfort — easy to make in bright fabrics with washable fillings. Cover old cushions in matching fabric to tone with your quilt, and throw piles of pillows across your bed, too. Splashes of contrasting colour look great as well — like the blue and yellow pillow shown here — and break up your basic colour.

If you're handy with the old needle and thread, appliqué bold shapes on to plain pillows — The Ed. made super sugar-pink ones with white clouds! If Dad's thinking of redecorating, choose white walls and add colour with cushions — or search out matching wallpaper and fabric for curtains for a co-ordinated look.

Little Extras!

Little things mean a lot, and a particular picture, poster or ornament can inspire you to revamp your room — rather like buying a suit to match a button!

The little yellow New York taxi — picked up cheaply from a junk shop — suggested a matching banana table bought from a gardening store, which in turn gave us the idea of splashing out on a yellow garden chair, too, for colour co-ordination.

A pretty, pop-up birthday card on a bed-side table adds interest, too, and if you're a collecter, make the most of your finds by displaying them on simple shelves or a low table. Old bottles, coloured glass or junk-shop gems catch the light when displayed near a window, and give a personal touch, too. Don't be afraid to give the occasional clue to the real you in your room — your hobbies, interests and favourite bits and pieces — for an individual touch. You're *you* — so let the real you shine through — and make your surroundings just as much a part of you, too!

The luckier ones among us have a knack for ferretting out second-hand finds for mere pennies — others need a gentle push in the right direction! Make regular trips to second-hand shops, though, and keep looking out for jumble sales or old odds and ends that Granny's throwing out. Keep your eyes peeled when you're shopping for the following items, too . . .
*A cork pinboard with a self-adhesive backing, or cork tiles held in place with self-adhesive strips.
*Coloured light bulbs for moody, subdued lighting.
*Plastic containers that held ice-cream, to label and use for storage — or tubs in bright shades used as kitchen tidies. Look out for screw-top jars and cutlery trays in the kitchen, too.
*Pieces of Thirties' coloured glass and junk-shop crockery.
*Second-hand mirrors and mirror tiles from do-it-yourself shops to give an illusion of space.
*Mobiles and wall-hangings from toy shops.
*Old tailors' dummies from junk shops — great to pile up with hats, scarves and accessories!

Let's hope we've sparked off a few bright ideas to smarten up your room — and whether you go for banana like us, pure white or sizzling orange, make sure *your* room's the place to be!

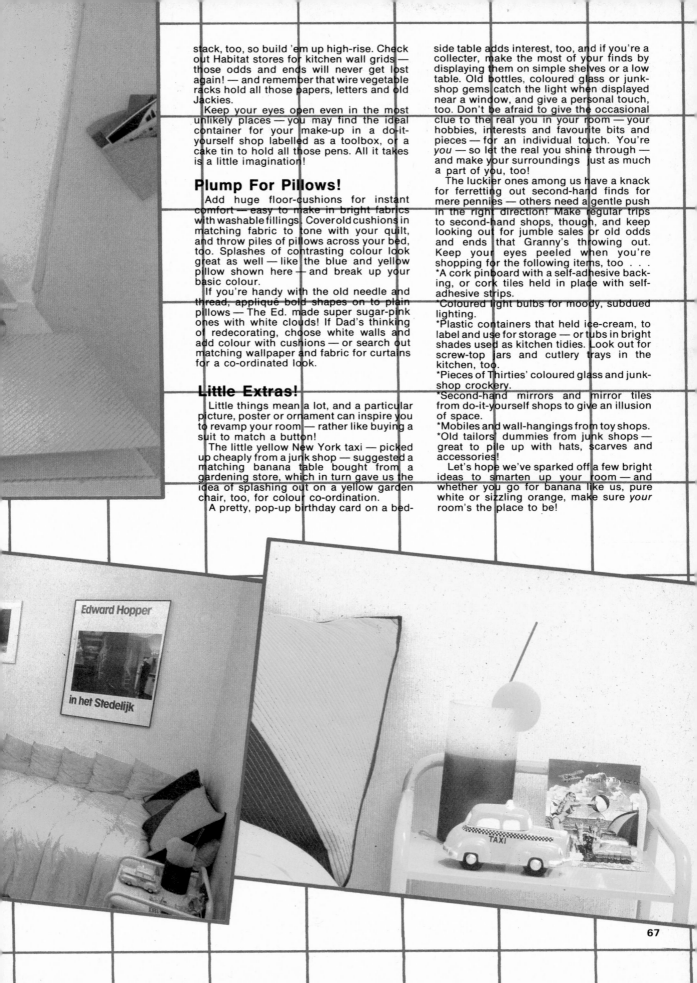

Edward Hopper in het Stedelijk

Mistaken Identity

A Short Story Specially Written For Jackie By Mary Hooper.

THAT dishy Jim rang,'' Julie said as soon as I got in from college. "He's coming to collect me at seven-fifteen."

I stared at her in silence and a thousand dreams crumbled around me.

"Collect *you*?" I repeated, trying to sound pleased for her. "How nice. Where's he taking you?"

"I didn't actually catch where it was — that phone in the hall is just awful. It's bound to be somewhere nice, though."

"Bound to be," I echoed, hoping I didn't sound bitter. Julie always got taken to nice places — she was that sort of girl. I was the sort who got a walk through the park and a hamburger at the end of it if I was lucky, and then only if I paid for it myself.

But Jim! For quite a lot of last night I'd kidded myself it was me he liked. We'd had quite a crowd round — most of them students from the tech, where I was doing a catering course and Julie was training to be a beautician. Even if you didn't know which of us was doing which course, one look was enough to tell you; I was the one with the bright red cheeks, scratchy hands and flour over her clothes, while Julie was the one with shiny hair, long lashes and three different shades of eyeshadow.

I hadn't been red or floury last night, though. I'd made sure of that. I'd made a big effort with my make-up and was doing my best to look party-ish. I'd enjoyed myself, too — especially after I'd met Jim.

I'd noticed him as soon as he'd arrived — with his looks, it'd be hard not to! — and my heart had done a triple somersault. He was the first boy I'd seen since coming to London that I'd really fancied. I mean, *really* fancied.

He'd come over to me, introduced himself, and without either of us actually asking, we started dancing. We got on really well too. He was new to London as well; had come up with his firm for a year's business experience.

We danced for ages and I was just beginning to think . . . to hope . . . that it might mean he was as interested in me as I was in him. But then Julie had spotted us together and pounced. We were short of boys, she said, something had gone wrong with the numbers, so would Jim mind circulating a bit and dancing with some of the other girls? Her first, naturally.

After that I might just as well have crawled into the kitchen and practised making flaky pastry. Julie fluttered about him, fixing him with coy, shy smiles and devious glances from under her lashes. He had been bewitched.

"What do you think of my party dress, Sammy?" Julie said now, holding up her emerald taffeta dress. "Or would that be a bit too much?" She flew to the window. "It's just starting to snow; I hope he doesn't want me to walk anywhere. Has he got a car, d'you think?"

"I don't know," I said gloomily. If you'd left him with me a bit longer I might have found out for you, I almost added, but stopped myself.

"Hmmmm . . ." She flung open her wardrobe. "Not my pink frilly skirt, I wore it last night. Not my black — it's too formal. Not . . ."

I glowered at her, but of course she was facing the other way and couldn't see me. It wasn't fair, though, it really wasn't. She could get anyone she wanted — and frequently did. Why couldn't she at least leave me Jim?

"What about Dave?" I asked her suddenly. "Doesn't he usually come round on Wednesdays?"

She waved a hand airily. "He must understand that I can't devote every Wednesday to him. If he arrives it's just too bad."

"Want me to make an excuse for you?" I asked sarcastically.

"Would you mind?" Julie asked, smiling gratefully.

I gritted my teeth. "Not at all," I answered, resisting the urge to scratch her eyes out.

She plunged into the wardrobe and came out with a red silky dress. "This, I think. I've got an idea he'll like me in red."

I smiled a tigerish sort of smile, teeth still gritted, but she didn't notice.

She wafted round the room, picking up things: perfume and hair spray and bath oil — and my red shoes. "You won't be going out, will you? They're the only ones that'll really go," she said at that point, before disappearing into the bathroom.

WHILE she was gone I managed to ungrit my teeth and set about tidying up the place. I'd be pleasant yet distant when Jim arrived, I decided. I'd hint in a subtle way that I might be doing something later and give no indication whatsoever that I'd ever thought there could have been anything between us.

And then, when they'd gone, I could storm around and kick things and throw Julie's teddy bear nightdress case on the floor to make myself feel better.

I changed into my scruffiest jeans and an old sweatshirt that had once been my brother's and was about fifteen sizes too large instead, just to show him that I hadn't made the slightest effort to look good for him.

After an hour and a half Julie reappeared, glistening and glowing, every visible part of her polished to perfection.

"If I could borrow your little red bag . . ." she said in a voice which implied she was actually doing me a favour in taking it somewhere. I went to find it and then when I was still half in and half out of the cupboard where it was lurking, Jim appeared.

He stood in the doorway, beaming at both of us.

Julie smiled graciously while I tried to flatten down my hair. "Sammy's just getting her red handbag for me," she said, "then I shall be all matching." She smoothed down the silky fabric and looked

coy, obviously waiting for a compliment.

"Very . . . er . . . nice," Jim said.

I looked at him in a careless sort of way, hoping he couldn't tell that my heart was being torn into about four hundred pieces. The heartless, callous beast! How could he just come round for Julie as if he hadn't been chatting me up half the evening? He might at least have had the decency to arrange to meet her outside somewhere.

"Now I'm all ready!" Julie trilled to Jim as I held out the bag.

Jim looked at her and smiled pleasantly. "You're obviously going out, too, are you? That's nice," he said.

I've heard of the term "stunned silence" before, but it was only then that I realised what it was like. The only movements in the room were my jaw and Julie's as they both dropped open.

"I . . . er . . ." Julie said after a moment.

"Perhaps Sammy and I can drop you somewhere — my car's outside," Jim continued, unaware of the bombshell he'd just dropped.

"No, I'm . . . he's . . ." Julie mumbled.

I found my voice. "I believe Dave's coming here, isn't he, Julie?"

She nodded and I was caught between wild elation and deep despair. Just *look* at the state of me!

Jim looked at his watch. "We're only going to the pictures but I think we'd better be off. Did I say on the phone that it starts at seven-thirty?"

"I — I couldn't hear all that well," I said timidly. "It was a bad line."

"You're not kidding! It sounded like I was speaking to a bowl of breakfast cereal."

I went to get my coat, and when I came back Jim was looking at me in a starry-eyed sort of way. I don't think he'd even noticed the sweatshirt and jeans. "Ready?" he said.

I nodded. He held out his hand and I took it. " 'Bye, Julie!" we chorused, and Julie had the grace to smile kindly at us, as if she was giving us both her blessing.

Well, I suppose it was all she *could* do, in the circumstances . . .

It simply wasn't fair. Julie was so pretty she could have any boy she wanted — and frequently did — so why couldn't she at least leave Jim for me?

Give Yourself A sporting Chance!

Exercise needn't be a chore — it should be *fun*, so don't torture yourself. Don't trudge out into the rain, tracksuit-clad, if pounding along the High Street's the last thing you'd rather be doing. Listen to your body and don't take on more than you can cope with — you're not in a competition for an Olympic medal and you don't have to prove anything.

There are lots of ways of keeping fit — some more strenuous than others — and there's bound to be something that's right up your street. So for a run-down on sporty suggestions — we've popped jogging in there, too! — read on!

PEDAL POWER!

You'll need: A bike, obviously — but if you're bikeless at the moment, why not find out about hiring one — enquire at your local cycle shop, or scan the second-hand ads in your local paper. Go for a bike with several speeds, as a five-speed cycle would make tackling those hills a lot less painful! Wear comfy sweat pants, tucked into socks if yours are extra-baggy ones that might trap in the chain. Invest in a saddle bag, too, to pack with goodies and a bottle of squash if you're heading off for the day.

Before you set off, check your tyres — not forgetting to take a pump with you — and make sure your lights are in working order. Pick up a cycling manual — it'll give you a run-down on all the safety checks to make.

Fitness Points

Cycling's a form of aerobic exercise — exercise that gives your heart, lungs and blood vessels a boost and strengthens them by providing a period of non-stop strenuous work. Cycling keeps leg muscles in trim, too, as well as refreshing a sluggish system.
CYCLING BURNS UP: 600 calories per hour.
FIGURE-SHAPING RATING: *
STRENGTH BUILD-UP RATING: ***
STAMINA BUILD-UP RATING: ****

JUST JOGGIN' ALONG!

You'll need: A good pair of running shoes, otherwise you'll risk injuring your feet and legs — so it's worth splashing out. There's no need to pay out for flashy jogging suits — a pair of shorts with an ancient sweatshirt would do the job just as well. Stick to natural fibres, though, otherwise you'll feel pretty hot and sticky after your run, and wrap up if the day's chilly. Tie your hair back and you're ready — and, hopefully, raring — to go!

Fitness Points

Always warm up before jogging — a five-minute stint of side-bends, stretches and toe-touches will loosen you up. At first, simply run till you feel a little tired, walk a distance and run again. You're not in a race, so simply jog a little faster than you'd walk, and you'll be amazed at how quickly you improve! Jogging gives your heart and lungs a spell of constant exercise, as well as keeping your legs and bottom in trim — and clearing those spots!
JOGGING BURNS UP: 700 calories per hour.
FIGURE-SHAPING RATING: **
STRENGTH BUILD-UP RATING: **
STAMINA BUILD-UP RATING: ****

IN THE SWIM!

You'll need: Simply, a swimming costume — and somewhere to swim! The only outlay's your admission fee to the pool, so find out about special rates for students or the unemployed — and enquire about buying a season ticket at a special, reduced rate. Get fit — on the cheap!

Fitness Points

You'll already know how relaxing a slow length or two of the pool can be — so let all those worries float away! Swimming's the best all-over toner, as every muscle in your body's given a work-out, whichever stroke you use. As with any form of exercise, gradually build up the number of lengths you tackle.
SWIMMING BURNS UP: 600 calories per hour.
FIGURE-SHAPING RATING: ***
STRENGTH BUILD-UP RATING: ****
STAMINA BUILD-UP RATING: ****

ON THE SPOT EXERCISES!

You'll need: Basically, a leotard, although a loose-fitting T-shirt and shorts would do the job. Pop on legwarmers with a bright leotard and enjoy looking good while you exercise — it's well worth treating yourself to give your ego a boost! There are lots of exercise tapes and records on the market — great to play when you get together with friends for a keep-fit session, but they're really not necessary and you could quite easily stretch to your favourite records or tapes. Music, incidentally, makes exercise — which can become a little tedious — much more enjoyable, and you'll find that you'll fall into a rhythm which makes those movements a lot less monotonous!

Fitness Points:

Remember to warm up by doing a few gentle bends and stretches, and give your body an all-over workout, concentrating on your problem areas. Don't expect overnight miracles, though, as it'll be at least a couple of months before you actually notice any difference — although it won't be long before you *feel* tons better!
ON-THE-SPOT EXERCISES BURN UP: 300-400 calories per hour, depending on how strenuously you exercise!
FIGURE-SHAPING RATING: ****
STRENGTH BUILD-UP RATING: *
STAMINA BUILD-UP RATING: **

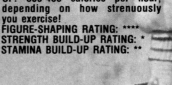

Curls, Curls, Curls !

Try out the following ideas and you'll never be bored with your hair again!

PIPE DREAMS!

To achieve a wrinkly, pre-Raphaelite cascade of curls, try this pipe cleaner method. You'll need about two packets of pipe cleaners if your hair is fairly long; they're quite cheap and available from newsagents and tobacconists or your dad, if he's a pipe smoker. (He won't need them once you've nagged him into giving up his pipe on account of his health!)

Bend each pipe cleaner in half, like a hoop, and plait two strands of hair round it, one strand to each leg of the loop (see photo). Twist the pipe cleaner round to secure the hair and repeat until you've plaited your whole head of hair. Leave to dry for a few hours or overnight before unpleating each pipe cleaner again. If you want your curls to last, spray them with a fine mist of hair spray and don't comb or brush your hair.

You'll achieve a similar effect without pipe cleaners if you make lots of little plaits all over your hair. Tie the ends of the plaits with wool to keep them in, but don't use elastic bands as they damage your hair. However, you'll probably find the pipe cleaner method is less fiddly.

RAG DOLL!

Binding up damp hair with rags has been done by generations of girls — ask your mum or granny! It takes several attempts before you discover the best way to wrap and tie your own particular hair for the end result you want, so practise plenty before you attempt to stun at a special occasion!

The way the girl in the photo has bound her hair will result in a full, bouncy head of hair rather than tight curls, because she's only tied up about half the length of each strand. So, if your shoulder-length or even jaw-length hair is looking rather lank and droopy, try this idea to put back its natural bounce.

First rip up some old soft cotton items of clothing to make your rags. You can sleep quite comfortably with your hair in rags but, if you tied your hair with attractive patterned cotton or rags, you could actually keep them in as you go about your business in the daytime — at weekends or holiday time, anyway!

To give the end result extra body, grab a section of wet hair and pull it in the opposite direction to the way you want it to lie and tie one knot or two in your rag as you tie it round. Carry on until all your hair is wrapped up.

Wait until your hair is dry then untie the rags and brush or comb your hair into the style you want.

Swap skirts for shawls for trousers
for tops — and come up with a look
that's all your own!

Winter

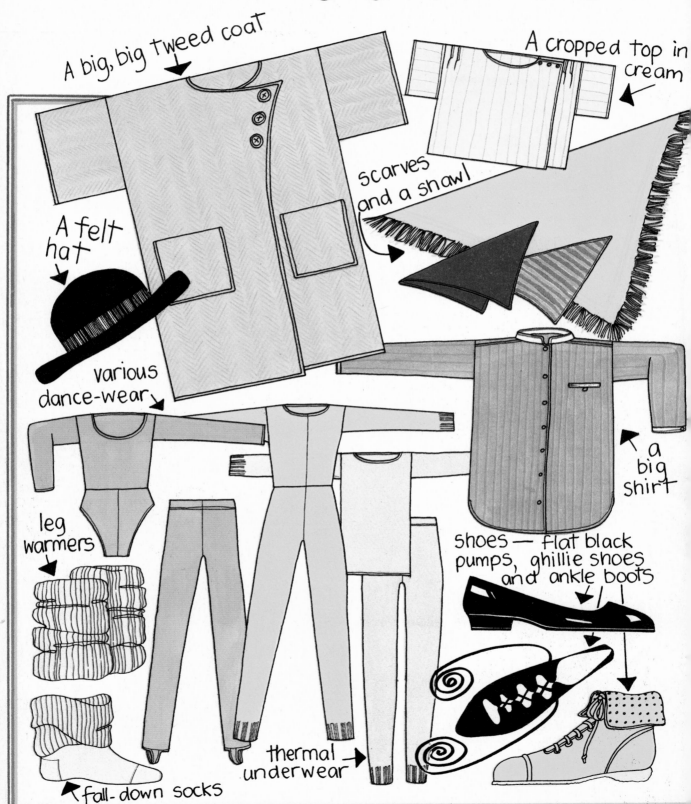

A big, big tweed coat

A cropped top in cream

A felt hat

scarves and a shawl

various dance-wear

a big shirt

leg warmers

shoes — flat black pumps, ghillie shoes and ankle boots

thermal underwear

fall-down socks

Wardrobe!

A cropped jacket in a natural fabric

A big dress—maybe linen or cord or fine wool

A big hand-knitted jumper

diamante jewellery

A frilly petticoat

belts

A full flannel skirt

A pleated skirt

cropped trousers

cropped jeans

A classic saddle-bag

Continued on page 74

Putting the look together ——

The coat is big - wear it over everything — don't worry about skirts hanging below the coat - it's a nice look!

The dress can be belted and worn over the skirts or trousers and dance-wear.

Wear fall-down socks and the hat and the petticoat-pile on the layers.

The cropped jacket goes over every-thing too.

Don't forget your diamante!

The cropped top with the skirt and the shawl as a belt on the hips —— roll a scarf for your neck.

Hat, scarves and diamanté with everything.

The scarf tied pirate style, add your diamanté — Belt the big shirt with the shawl over the skirt or the trousers.

Dance - wear goes under everything.

The belted jumper with the pleated skirt is a smarter look.

The dress over jeans and petticoat with ghillie shoes looks nice.

Work out your own combinations!

The Boy Next Door

Well I didn't ask you! And I wish you'd stop interfering in my life!

Don't be silly, Norma. It was an accident. And I did you a favour getting rid of him.

Yes—well—I suppose he was a bit creepy really. And how dare he call Glen a mangy mutt.

That's better. You should listen to me, you know! After all, I have lived next door to you for sixteen years.

That's true. But you must admit that just lately, you have been getting to be a bit of a pest.

Me? What have I done?

Remember Steve?

I don't want to share you with anyone else, Norma. I want you all to myself.

Oh, Steve, what a nice thing to say.

Norma! Hi there!

idiot! You fool! Look what you've done!

I'm sorry. It was an accident.

The funny thing was, Steve turned really nasty then, and I wasn't all that sorry to see him go.

I could have told you that. I know Steve Jones. He's got a rotten temper.

Yes, OK, so your accident saved me from a fate worse than death. But what about Neville? You got rid of him, too.

Remember?

He's super, Dave. Very serious. He writes poems. He's written one about me. Can you imagine that?

He sounds a right wet. And I bet his poems are rubbish.

But no-one got a chance to find out, because . . .

I'll read you my poem now, Norma. I think you'll agree it's very good.

Yes, Neville. Please go ahead.

77

Then you came along . . .

Aah! Stop it! I'm all wet!

Sorry, mate. But I couldn't agree more.

Dave! You—you idiot! I hate you!

You must admit, though, it was funny.

Yes, I suppose it was. And he was wet!

Then, a few days later . . .

What are you all dressed up for? Going somewhere special?

It just so happens I'm going out with Colin Stone.

And I don't want you coming near us with any hoses or hairy dogs. Is that clear?

You're never going out with Colin Stone. He's a dangerous person for little girls like you to know. Honestly, Norma, don't get involved with him.

Dave, I know all about Colin's reputation and I can handle him. And besides, I'm not a little girl any more.

Anyone could tell Dave didn't approve, though.

Hi, Norma. Still going out with Casanova, are you? Remember what I told you about him.

Hi, Dave. Now push off, will you, or Norma will start to believe what you're telling her.

He didn't give up, though.

So Colin didn't turn up last night, eh? I told you what he's like.

He didn't turn up because he had to go and see his gran. He told me. And I believe him.

More fool you, then. I bet he was out with another girl.

He was not! And don't you dare say those things about him!

I just don't want you to get hurt, Norma, that's all.

Dave! Stop it! You're spilling oil on me!

I'm sorry, Norma. I'm really sorry.

Stay away from me! Just stay away from me! I like Colin and you're not going to turn me against him. You've destroyed everything I've ever had with anyone else but I'm not going to let you ruin things between me and Colin!

I don't ruin things on purpose, Norma. And Colin Stone is a two-timing creep as far as girls are concerned. Believe me.

I'm not going to listen to any more of this. And I think you do ruin things on purpose! You just don't want me to be happy, Dave Kidd!

THAT'S RIDICULOUS. OF COURSE I WANT HER TO BE HAPPY. BUT—MAYBE I WANT HER TO BE HAPPY WITH—WITH ME . . .

AND—MAYBE I DID RUIN THINGS FOR HER ON PURPOSE. MAYBE I DON'T WANT HER TO GO OUT WITH ANYONE ELSE BECAUSE—BECAUSE I WANT HER TO GO OUT WITH ME.

BUT I COULDN'T EVER TELL HER HOW I FEEL. SHE JUST SEES ME AS THE BOY NEXT DOOR—AND A PRETTY ANNOYING ONE AT THAT. I THINK I'LL JUST KEEP OUT OF HER WAY IN FUTURE. SHE'LL BE MUCH HAPPIER THAT WAY . . .

But a few days later . . .

Dave, I think you've been avoiding me, so I've come to say I'm sorry I shouted at you and can we still be friends. Please?

Oh, yes, sure, Norma, of course we can. And I admit I have been a bit of a pest. I promise I won't interfere again.

Good. That's OK then. Now come on and I'll buy you a Coke. If you promise not to spill it all over me.

Em—no, Norma. I-I've got some work to do. Some other time, OK?

Oh—yes, OK, Dave.

SOMETHING'S WRONG. HE'S DIFFERENT SOMEHOW. I SHOULDN'T HAVE BEEN SO NASTY TO HIM. IT WASN'T HIS FAULT.

And, back home . . .

OH DAVE, I'VE CRIED ON YOUR SHOULDER A HUNDRED TIMES AND YOU'VE BRIGHTENED A HUNDRED ROTTEN DAYS. WE USED TO BE SUCH GOOD FRIENDS, BUT I'VE GONE AND SPOILT IT ALL. THINGS'LL NEVER BE THE SAME BETWEEN US AGAIN . . .

They didn't see much of each other until a few days later . . .

Oh, Dave. Hi. Em—Mum wonders if she could borrow that knitting pattern?

Oh—yes—sure. I'll find it for you. Mum left it out before she went shopping.

Here it is.

Thanks, Dave. And—I—I'm sorry things don't seem the same between us any more. It—it's not because of Colin, is it?

Don't be silly, Norma. It's—well, it's difficult to explain, but—

But what, Dave?

Norma—Oh, Norma, I—

But just then . . .

Hello, dear. Get the knitting pattern, did you?

Em . . . yes—yes I did. I-I'm just going now, Mrs Kidd. Bye then, Dave.

DAVE WAS DIFFERENT THIS AFTERNOON. I WONDER WHAT HE WAS GOING TO SAY TO ME? AND—AND WHY DID I FEEL SO STRANGE WHEN HE LOOKED AT ME THAT WAY? IT—IT WAS ALMOST AS THOUGH I WANTED HIM TO KISS ME.

OF ALL THE BOYS I'VE EVER KNOWN, DAVE'S THE ONE I'VE ALWAYS GOT ON BEST WITH. AND— I REALLY DID WANT HIM TO KISS ME.

BUT IT'S SILLY TO THINK LIKE THIS. HE ONLY SEES ME AS A FRIEND. AND BESIDES, I'M GOING TO THIS PARTY TONIGHT WITH COLIN.

And at the party . . .

Dave! You didn't tell me you were invited to Meg's party.

To tell you the truth. I'd forgotten all about it. Then I decided to come along. Are—are you here with Colin?

Yes. There he is. And that girl's just—just a friend, he says.

Yeah, they look really friendly to me. Look, Norma, I know I said I wouldn't interfere, but I just don't want to see you get hurt, that's all.

IS THAT ALL, DAVE? I DON'T KNOW WHY, BUT SOMEHOW I WANT IT TO BE MORE THAN THAT . . .

Hey, Norma. You're with me, remember?

Then Dave came over.

Well, Colin, still going out with Norma, then?

For the moment. But there's nothing serious about it. There are far too many other girls around for me to start getting serious about one!

And later . . .

I HOPE YOU DON'T GET HURT, NORMA. BUT IF YOU DO, I'LL ALWAYS BE HERE FOR YOU. I'LL COMFORT YOU AND DRY YOUR TEARS AND YOU'LL NEVER, EVER KNOW HOW I REALLY FEEL ABOUT YOU . . .

Look, some of my mates have just come in. Hang on. I want to speak to them.

Sure . . . OK.

Continued on page 86

What did he mean by that?

When it comes to dealing with boys, one of the things to remember is that they don't always say what they mean. It can take a lot of time and practice to break through the language barrier and find out what they're really thinking, so to speed things up a bit, here's our fun look at some of the things a boy might say to you—and what he really means . . .

YOUR FIRST DATE

What he says
" It's a great evening. Fancy walking to the disco?"
What he means
" I know it's freezing and about to rain, but I could only get £5 off my dad and the bus fare's 50p each into town."
Or he could say
" Aren't you taking a bag or something?"
And what he means is
" If you're not taking a bag, that means you're not taking a purse and that means you're not taking any money. And I've only got a fiver."

AT THE DISCO

He says
" Let's sit in the corner. It's far quieter over there."
What he means is
" It's really dark in the corner. Let's go and have a necking session."
Or, if you're very unlucky, he could mean
" It's really dark in the corner. With any luck my mates won't see me with you over there."
When he wants to impress, he'll say
" Great record, huh? I know that group pretty well."
What he means is
" I once sent them a song I'd written and they sent it back asking me to try again in five years' time."

WHEN YOU'VE BEEN SEEING EACH OTHER FOR A WHILE

He'll say
" I phoned you last night and you weren't in."
What he means is,
" Someone told me you went out with Steve Smith last night. Did you?"
Or he'll say
" Me? Go out with Brenda Jones? Don't be silly! Who told you that?"
What he means is
" How did you find out about me and Brenda? I bet it was that so-called mate of mine. Was it him?"

WHEN HE WANTS TO DROP YOU IN FAVOUR OF BRENDA JONES

He'll say
" I think we should stop seeing each other for a week or two. That'll give us a chance to find out what we really feel about each other."
What he means is
" I want to go out with Brenda Jones. But just in case things don't work out, I want to make sure you'll still be around."
Or he'll say
" I like you too much to lie to you."
What he means is
" I'm too much of a coward to tell you the truth, so there's no way I'm going to mention Brenda Jones. I wonder if you'll believe me if I tell you I'm going to join the Foreign Legion?"
Or he could say
" I think we're getting too involved, too soon."
And what he'll mean is,
" I want to go out with Brenda Jones."

WHEN HE WANTS YOU TO BE HIS GIRL

He'll say
" My brother's coming home in four months. You'll like him."
What he means is
" I want you to know I'd still like to be going out with you in four months. And besides that, I want you to meet my family."
Or he'll say
" I really like you a lot. More than I've ever liked any girl."
What he means is
" I think I love you."
Or he could say,
" I love you."
And what he'll more than likely mean is
" I love you!"

Stitch up your wardrobe by knitting yourself a pattern to be proud of! It's easy to knit, easy to wear and easy on your pocket — so what are you waiting for?

MATERIALS

9 (10, 10) 50 g balls PINGOUIN PINGOSTAR in Main Shade (MS). 1 ball in each of three contrast shades. Pair each 3¾ mm and 4½ mm (Nos. 9 and 7) needles.

MEASUREMENTS

To fit bust: 86 (91, 96) cms [34 (36, 38) ins.]
Sleeve seam: 43 (44.5, 46) cms [17 (17½, 18) ins.]

TENSION

20 sts and 26 rows to 10 cms (4 ins.) measured over st-st using 4¼ mm needles.

ABBREVIATIONS

K — knit; P — purl; st(s) — stitch(es); st-st — stocking-stitch; inc — increase; dec — decrease; rep — repeat; cont — continue; rem — remain(ing); alt — alternate; beg — beginning; foll — following; MS — Main Shade; A — 1st Contrast; B — 2nd Contrast; C — 3rd Contrast; cms — centimetres; ins — inches.

BACK

Using 3¾ mm needles, cast on 84 (90, 96) sts and work 7 cms (3 ins.) in K1, P1 rib.
Change to 4½ mm needles and work 6 rows in st-st. Now work from Chart. Work 10th to 22nd rows then work 1st to 7th rows. Cont in st-st in MS until work measures 43 (45, 47) cms (16, 17, 17½) ins. Now work from 1st to 32nd rows, then 8th to 22nd rows. Start neck at front, then work 1st to 7th rows of Chart, omitting spots at armhole edges.
At the same time on the 3rd row of pattern Shape Armholes, keeping pattern correct — *Cast off 3 sts at beg of next 4 rows.
Dec 1 st at each end of next 3 rows * . ** [66 (72, 78) sts] Cont in st-st in MS until Armhole measures 19 (20.5, 22) cms (7½ (8, 8½) ins).
Shape Shoulders — Cast off 5 (6, 6) sts at beg of next 8 (4, 8) rows. Cast off 0 (5, 0) sts at beg of next 0 (4, 0) rows. Leave rem 26 (28, 30) sts on a spare needle for band.

FRONT

Work as for Back to **.
Shape Neck.
1st row —Patt 28 (30, 32),

Continued On Page 84.

USE YOUR LOAF...
and lose some weight!

From top left clockwise – Borsch, Consomme, Hungarian Sausage and Tomato and Creamy Leek and Courgette.

If you love sandwiches but need to lose weight try our souper sandwich diet.

SANDWICH SUPER SNACK!

You may be able to take a packed lunch with you to school but if you have a filling canteen lunch have a sandwich snack for your evening meal instead.

MAIN MEAL

Whether you eat this in the school canteen or at home, try to avoid fattening extras or fried dishes and go for lean meats and green vegetables.

GOOD MORNING GRUB!

Start with fresh fruit or fruit juice, then have a slice of Slimcea, toasted if you like, with a little low-calorie margarine plus ONE of the following —

1 fruit yoghurt
1 oz. cereal with ½ cupful low-fat milk
2 slices lean bacon and grilled tomatoes
1 egg boiled, poached or scrambled
3 oz. portion grilled fish
2 well-grilled sausages with grilled mushrooms

MAIN MEAL

You could start with clear soup, melon, grapefruit, fruit juice or tomato salad. Then eat a 4 oz. portion of any lean meat or 6-8 oz. grilled fish with at least two green vegetables and a small helping of *one* of the following: boiled or jacket potato, sweetcorn, mashed swede or boiled brown rice.

Finish with an apple or orange or a cup of tea or coffee.

SOUP AND SANDWICH SNACK

Have one serving of one of the soups and a sandwich made from 2 slices of white or brown Slimcea bread (30 cals. per slice, lightly buttered with low-calorie margarine) and one of the listed fillings. Drink tea or coffee sweetened with an artificial sweetener.

SOUP RECIPES

These recipes serve 4, so Mum can make them for the whole family!

CREAMY LEEK AND COURGETTE — Wash **4 medium leeks** and **½ lb. courgettes**, then trim off the ends and slice them thinly. Place them in a medium-sized saucepan with **1 pint low-calorie milk** and bring to the boil. Season and simmer for 20 minutes until the vegetables are soft. Puree in a blender or sieve and re-heat. Serve with grated carrot sprinkled on top of each bowlful.

100 cals. per serving.

BORSCH — Peel **1 lb. cooked beetroot** and dice. Dissolve **2 teaspoonfuls Bovril** in ¼ pint hot water. Add beetroot to liquid together with juice of **1 lemon**, ½ small **onion**, sliced, 4 tablespoonfuls **cider** or **wine vinegar**, salt and pepper to taste and 6 tablespoonfuls of **natural yoghurt**. Blend half the above until smooth, then repeat with remainder and put both parts together. You can serve this soup chilled or re-heat it.

80 cals. per serving.

CONSOMME — Put 3 dessertspoonfuls of **Bovril**, 1½ pints water, a large bay leaf, ½ teaspoonful each thyme and marjoram, 1 large **onion**, peeled and diced, and 2 **carrots**, peeled and sliced, into a saucepan and bring slowly to the boil. Lower heat, cover and simmer for 1 hour. Strain the liquid and return to pan, add some small pieces of vegetable such as broccoli, red pepper and mushrooms, a dessertspoonful of lemon juice and salt and pepper to taste. Simmer gently for about ten minutes.

100 cals. per serving (approx.).

HUNGARIAN SAUSAGE AND TOMATO SOUP — Fry 1 chopped **green pepper** with 1 chopped **onion** in a little fat in a non-stick pan, add 2 level dessertspoonfuls of **paprika,** and 2 tablespoonfuls of **tomato puree.** Gradually blend in 1½ pints of **stock** made with 2 red Bovril cubes and cook, stirring continuously, until the soup boils. Lower heat and add an 8 oz. can of **frankfurters**, chopped into small rounds, and simmer for half an hour. Serve each portion topped with a dessertspoonful of **natural yoghurt.**

Approx. 120 cals. per serving.

SLIMWICHES

Slimwiches, just like sandwiches, can be served in an infinite variety of ways: with white bread or brown, toasted or not, open, closed or layered.

The giant sandwich shown here is filled as follows from top to bottom — tomato and cucumber, tuna in brine with lettuce, scrambled egg and watercress, pressed chicken, ham, red peppers and coriander, cottage cheese and prawns and lettuce and tomato.

Here are some calorie counted ideas —

2 oz. cottage cheese mixed with a little grated apple	111
2 oz. prawns and cucumber	135
1 hard-boiled egg and chopped gherkins	151
1 oz. drained salmon and chopped spring onions	110
2 sliced grilled kidneys and scrambled egg	253
4 oz. grilled mushroom and watercress	119

(These calorie ratings allow for ¼ oz. low-calorie spread in each sandwich and 2 slices of Slimcea bread.)

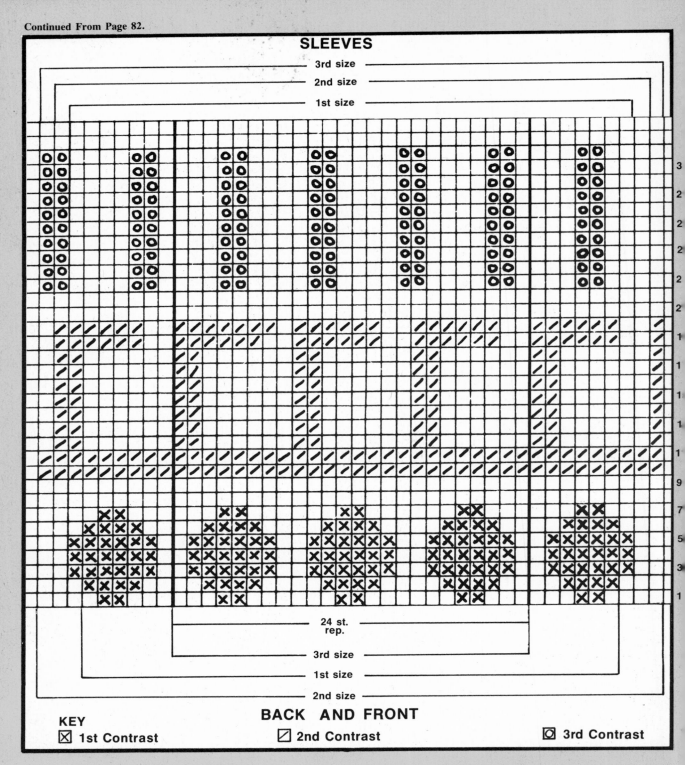

SLEEVES

3rd size

2nd size

1st size

3
2
2
2
2
1
1
1
1
9
7
5
3
1

24 st. rep.

3rd size

1st size

2nd size

BACK AND FRONT

KEY

⊠ 1st Contrast   ◪ 2nd Contrast   ◲ 3rd Contrast

---

turn. Patt 1 row. *Dec 1 st at neck edge on next 8 rows and then work straight until Armhole measures as Back ending at armhole edge.

Shape Shoulders — Cast off 5 (6, 6) sts at beg of next 4 (2, 4) alt rows, then 0 (5, 0) sts at beg of next 2 rows. Slip centre 10 (12, 14) sts onto a spare needle, then work other side to match reversing shapings.

SLEEVES
Using 3¾ mm needles, cast on 38 (40, 42) sts and work 5 cms (2 ins) in K1, P1 rib.
Change to 4½ mm needles and work 10th to 20th rows from Chart. Break A and join in MS, at the same time inc 1 st at each end of every 6th row to 64 (66, 68) sts.
Work straight until Sleeve measures 43 (44.5, 46) cms [17 (17½, 18) ins)] then shape

Armholes as on Back from * to *.
Dec 1 st at each end of every alt row to 36 sts, then dec 1 st at each end of every row to 20 sts. Cast off.
Sew up 1 shoulder seam and using 3¾ mm needles, pick up and K 78 (82, 86) sts evenly round neck.

NECKBAND
Work in K1, P1 rib for ⸱.5 cms

(1 in.). Cast off in rib using 4½ mm needles.

MAKE UP
Sew 2nd shoulder seam and neckband. Sew side and sleeve seams. Set in sleeves.

For details of your nearest Pingouin wool shop, send an s.a.e. to Stockist Queries, French Wools Ltd., 7-11 Lexington St., London W1R 4BU.

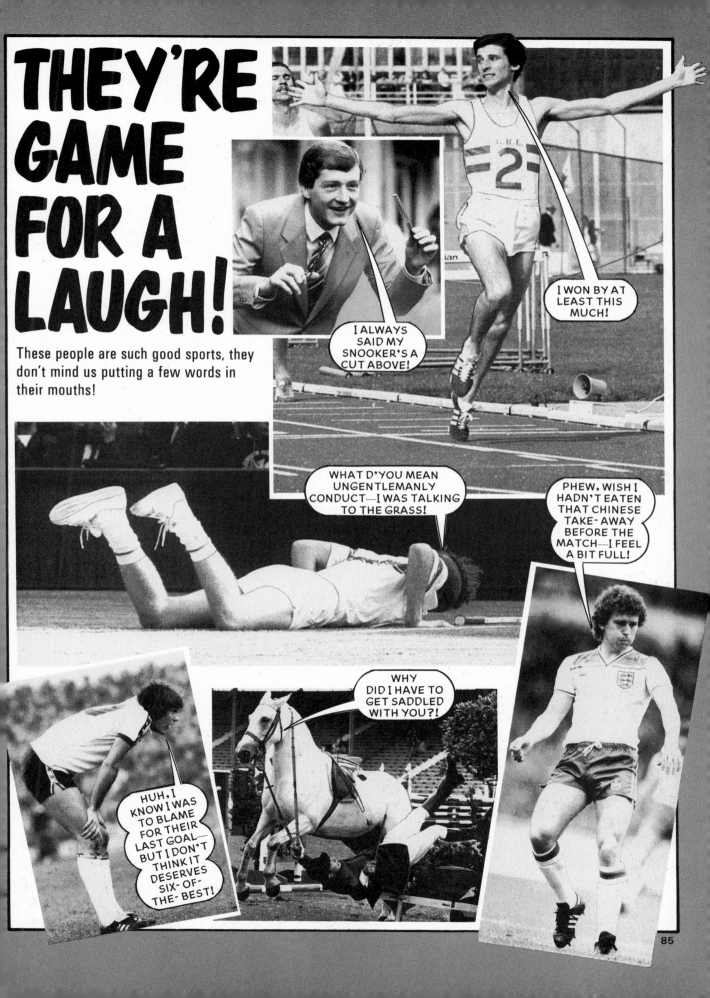

THEY'RE GAME FOR A LAUGH!

These people are such good sports, they don't mind us putting a few words in their mouths!

I ALWAYS SAID MY SNOOKER'S A CUT ABOVE!

I WON BY AT LEAST THIS MUCH!

WHAT D'YOU MEAN UNGENTLEMANLY CONDUCT—I WAS TALKING TO THE GRASS!

PHEW, WISH I HADN'T EATEN THAT CHINESE TAKE-AWAY BEFORE THE MATCH—I FEEL A BIT FULL!

WHY DID I HAVE TO GET SADDLED WITH YOU?!

HUH, I KNOW I WAS TO BLAME FOR THEIR LAST GOAL—BUT I DON'T THINK IT DESERVES SIX-OF-THE-BEST!

Continued from page 80

He was gone for ages.

HE'S IN NO GREAT HURRY TO COME BACK TO ME, THAT'S OBVIOUS.

He did come back for a dance, though . . .

WHO'S SHE, I WONDER? AND— AND WHY DO I WISH I WAS DANCING WITH DAVE INSTEAD OF COLIN?

Gosh, it's hot in here. How about grabbing us a couple of Cokes, Norma, while I speak to this friend of mine.

Oh . . . OK.

I KNOW HE'S TRYING TO GET OFF WITH THAT GIRL, BUT SOMEHOW I DON'T CARE.

And on the way back with the Cokes . . .

I CARE MORE ABOUT DAVE AND THE GIRL HE'S GETTING OFF WITH. LOOK AT HER, ACTING AS THOUGH SHE OWNED HIM.

Then it happened . . .

Aah! You—you idiot! You've spilled Coke all over me!

You clumsy fool! You ought to have a danger sign attached to you!

I-I'm sorry. It was an accident.

Yes, she didn't do it on purpose.

Norma! You clumsy twit! Where are our Cokes? You'll just have to get Kate and me two more.

Wh-what? I don't understand.

Look, I was going to tell you later, but since you ask, this is Kate. We've been seeing each other for a while now. So be a good girl and go and get us two more Cokes, OK?

Get your own Cokes, you creep!

HOW COULD HE? HOW COULD HE DO THAT TO ME IN FRONT OF EVERYONE? I'VE MADE A COMPLETE FOOL OF MYSELF. I'VE GOT TO GET OUT OF HERE!

And outside . . .

I'M—I'M NOT EVEN CRYING FOR COLIN. IT'S DAVE I CARE ABOUT. BUT—HE'S GOT A NEW GIRL NOW AND HE SAW ME MAKE A COMPLETE IDIOT OF MYSELF. I'LL NEVER HAVE A CHANCE WITH HIM NOW. NOT EVER . . .

Norma! Wait!

IT MUST BE COLIN. I SHOULD BE PLEASED, BUT I'M NOT. I-I WISH IT WAS DAVE.

I'LL TELL HIM I DON'T WANT TO SEE HIM ANY MORE. AND HE MUSTN'T KNOW I'VE BEEN CRYING. HE'LL THINK IT'S BECAUSE OF HIM.

Colin, I-I don't know how to say this, but—

Norma, it's not Colin. It's me, Dave. And, oh, Norma, please don't cry. Not over Colin. He's not worth it.

Dave! I-I'm not crying over Colin. I'm crying because—because—

Because of me, maybe? When you spilled that Coke, I thought maybe you felt the same way about me as I do about you.

You—you mean, you don't think it was an accident? And you mean, you—you feel the same way about me?

'Course I do, you idiot . . .

OH, DAVE . . .

But—what about that girl you were with?

Oh, her. It was more like she was with me. I kept telling her I wasn't interested but she wouldn't go away. Then when you spilled that Coke on her and she turned nasty, it gave me an excuse to get away.

But nobody'll dare come between us again. Because if they do—

We'll let dogs jump on them—

And squirt hoses at them!

And spill Coke over them—

THE END

ARIES

At your best, you're full of energy, honest, brave and strong. But at your worst, you can be quick-tempered, impatient, selfish and bossy. You have to be first in everything—the lunch queue, exams, work, relationships. You want everything now and you barge through life making sure you get it. You can be courageous and adventurous, but you can also be just plain aggressive and bad-tempered. You never think before you speak and for this reason you are not the ideal person to trust with secrets!

TAURUS

You can be practical, reliable and warm-hearted. But you can also be stodgy and self-centred and so stuck in a rut that it's difficult to see your way out of it. At your worst, you hate change and are stubborn enough to stick to your opinions no matter what. (You still think there should only be one television channel.) As far as boys are concerned, you're faithful, warm-hearted—and possessive. If your boyfriend so much as glances in another girl's direction, you'll be in a bad mood for a fortnight!

GEMINI

You're so lively, witty and attractive that you just can't help being a two-timing flirt as well! And you get away with it because you're so cunning and convincing. You can be caught entwined with your boyfriend's best mate and still manage to convince them both that you were only testing out your theory that your boyfriend kisses better than any other boy you know. You find it difficult to stick with anything. Once something new appears on the horizon—a new hobby, a new friend, a new boy—you drop all your old interests.

CANCER

Basically, you're kind, sensitive and sympathetic. But if things aren't going right for you, you can be over-emotional, touchy and moody. You're also an expert at harbouring grudges. People can go for months trying to figure out what it is they've done to offend you. You'll never tell them, though, because you think they should instinctively know what's wrong. And it could well be you've taken offence because they've told you you should tidy up your desk/room/handbag, because you do have the reputation for being one of the most untidy signs of the zodiac!

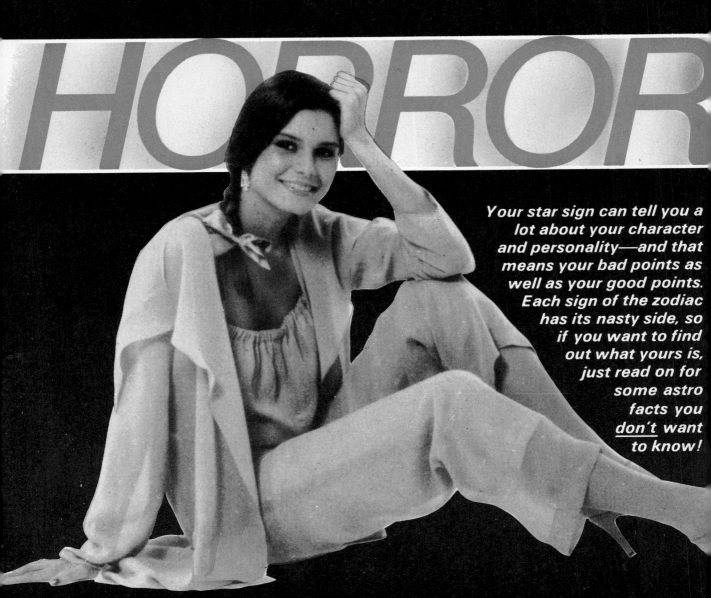

HORROR

Your star sign can tell you a lot about your character and personality—and that means your bad points as well as your good points. Each sign of the zodiac has its nasty side, so if you want to find out what yours is, just read on for some astro facts you don't want to know!

LEO

You're attractive and popular and everybody's sunshine girl—and don't you know it! You just want to spread happiness wherever you go. The trouble is, if other people don't want to fall in with your plans for them, you feel it's your duty to step in and organise their dull, boring little lives for them. You can't help being popular, but you might be a bit more popular if you stopped thinking you were doing people a favour by talking to them. And hard though it might be for you, you <u>could</u> step out of the spotlight once or twice—even if it's only for a few moments!

VIRGO

You're the modest, hard-working, helpful sign of the zodiac. The trouble is, if you're not careful, you can end up being picky, fussy and over-critical. You have to remember that cleaning the cooker and tidying out the hall cupboard isn't everyone's idea of a fun evening. You also tend to worry too much. You worry about your clothes, your hair, your health, other people's health, and if you can't find anything to worry about, you worry about not worrying. You'll never admit to any of this, though, because Virgos love to pretend they're perfect!

LIBRA

You're the nicest, sweetest, most tactful person around. The trouble is, you're so tactful and so anxious not to give offence, you end up being totally ignored. You take so many sides in a quarrel, no-one's got a clue what you actually do think. And after a while, you don't either. You tend to put off making decisions, too, and end up having them made for you. You rely on friends to tell you what to wear, where to go and who to go there with. If you ever do decide you want something, though, you usually end up getting it, one way or another!

SCORPIO

You have powerful feelings and emotions and unfortunately, one of the most powerful is your jealousy. Scorpios are Jealous. You're jealous if your friend gets better exam marks than you; you're jealous if your sister gets a bigger slice of cake than you; you're even jealous if the cat gets to sleep in your chair. And if your boyfriend dares to talk to another girl, they'll both feel the sting of your sharp Scorpio personality. You're stubborn, secretive and suspicious, but you're fascinating and there will always be something exciting going on when you're around!

SCOPES!

SAGITTARIUS

You love freedom and adventure and you're in your element striding fearlessly into unknown dangers. Unfortunately, you can end up striding fearlessly into other people's lives. You're one of the most tactless signs of the zodiac and if anyone's going to tell their best friend her new haircut makes her look like Worzel Gummidge, it's going to be you. You tend to exaggerate, too, and you can make deciding between having your chips with or without vinegar seem as difficult as trying to decide which outfit to wear to a Royal Garden party

CAPRICORN

You see yourself as reliable, careful and self-disciplined. But other people may just think you're being over-practical and disapproving. You can be a bit self-righteous and at your worst, will lecture your friends about what they should be doing with their lives instead of—horrors—enjoying themselves. Just because you think it's your duty to sit at home of an evening sorting out your parents' gas bill, it doesn't mean your friends are complete wastrels because they'd rather go to the movies. It's actually fun to do something mad and daft once in a while. Try it!

AQUARIUS

If there's a cause to be fought for or a wrong to be righted, you'll be the first to lend a hand, so long as there's no emotional commitment. You'd rather be working to Save the Whale than working on your relationships. You also always hate and disapprove of what the majority of people like to do. This means that you can spend many lonely evenings making Save the Whale T-shirts out of recycled string while your frinds are all enjoying themselves at the disco. Of course if everyone were to start making string T-shirts, you'd be off to the disco like a shot!

PISCES

You're sympathetic, sweet and kind. You just hate being nasty to anyone, and this means that you spend your time being nice to the nastiest, weediest people around. You're so busy being nice to other people, in fact, you forget how to run your own life and end up becoming totally dependent. If you don't get total emotional support from friends and boyfriends, you can whine on and on until you do. In fact, at your very worst, you can end up being a real drag. Try being genuinely, honestly, nasty once in a while. You'll be a nicer person for it!

Most boys are nice most of the time. No boy is perfect, but some boys are just plain *bad* and if you're unlucky enough to get involved with a bad boy, you're right in line to find out why so many love songs are sad songs.

Think you're too smart to fall for a bad boy? Think again! A bad boy's greatest asset is that he can attract girls the way a spider attracts flies. And he's just as deadly. So don't get caught in his trap. Learn to spot a bad boy before he gets the chance to capture — and break — your heart.

WARNING!
These Boys Are Dangerous !

DANGER!

The Bad Boy who won't take No for an answer.

This bad boy is probably the most dangerous of all. He's charming, tender and romantic, but his one aim with girls is to go a lot further than just kissing and cuddling. And if you say "No," he's got a whole arsenal of speeches already prepared and all guaranteed to break down your defences.

He'll tell you you're not a couple of kids any more . . . he'll tell you that for him this is the real thing . . . he'll let you know there have been other girls in his life — girls who weren't afraid like you . . .

And if you like him, which you most probably will, since this type of boy is usually popular and attractive, you'll listen to him.

Even though you know all about his reputation, you'll persuade yourself, with a little help from him, that you're different from all those other girls. You'll think this really is the real thing for him and that he really is in love with you, so what harm can it do?

The answer is an awful lot.

And if you think he really does love you, ask yourself why he's trying to push you to take decisions you feel are wrong for you.

Any boy who tries to cash in on emotional blackmail like this is bad news. If he won't listen to your opinions, respect your ideas and trust you to know what's right for *you*, he's a candidate for our bad boys line-up.

Beware of the boy who pushes you too far, who threatens to drop you "unless." A boy who cares about you will want decisions about the physical side of your relationship to be mutual ones.

But the bad boy doesn't care about you at all. He's out to get his own way and he'll threaten to walk out on you if he doesn't. And if, against your better judgment, you're silly enough to give in to him, he'll walk out on you anyway.

To a bad boy like this, a relationship means proving himself. Proving he can get any girl he wants. And once the challenge is gone — he is, too.

DANGER!

The Bad Boy who wants to take over your life.

He walks into your life and everything is suddenly beautiful. He really loves you. He's fascinated by everything about you — your hair, your clothes, the new shoes you bought . . .

He takes so much interest in you, in fact, that pretty soon he's suggesting what you ought to wear when he takes you out. He's also considerate enough to point out all the little faults you have.

So you wear the clothes he likes you to wear, you go to the places he wants you to go, you think the way he wants you to think, and you end up being completely dominated by him.

And when the dominating bad boy

does tell you it's over, you spend a long time wondering why. Didn't you try to be everything he wanted in a girl? Didn't you dress the way he liked and talk the way he liked and think the way he liked?

Yes, you did — and that was your mistake.

Beware of the boy who tries to do all your thinking for you and tries to turn you into someone else. If a relationship founders on the colour of a dress or the kind of records you like listening to, it isn't much of a relationship. And if a boy is attracted enough to ask you out in the first place why would he want to change you?

The boy who does is more than likely a little bit selfish and insecure and isn't ready for a relationship based on mutual give and take.

So don't make the mistake of allowing some boy to tell you what to think and how to dress. Nice boys will accept you as you are and won't try to change you. Bad boys won't.

DANGER!

The Bad Boy who'll two, three and even four-time you.

This particular bad boy finds it easy — too easy — to attract girls, and he finds them impossible to resist. He just adores being adored.

And the trouble is, he's just so easy to fall in love with. He'll tell you he really loves you back, too, and while he's saying it he probably means it. And he probably means it when he whispers exactly the same thing to Karen, Lucy, Annette or Hazel . . .

The two-timer is superb. When you eventually catch him out, it's more likely

to be because he wanted you to. Then, you see, he doesn't have to go through all the trouble involved in breaking off a relationship when he's tired of it.

All he has to do is let himself be caught out a few times and, what do you know, *you* do all the work for him! You send him packing.

Then, of course, you spend the next few weeks wondering why it was you packed up a boy you were crazy about. Maybe you should have forgiven him . . . maybe there's still time . . . maybe you should be more broad minded about these things . . . maybe he's really nice underneath it all . . .

Well, he's not! He's attractive and fun and great to be with, but he's also a grade one Bad Boy.

DANGER!

The Bad Boy who pretends you don't exist.

Unlike the two-timer, this bad boy needs, and wants, just one steady girlfriend. He likes having a steady girlfriend in the background. The trouble is, in the background is strictly where you'll stay.

When he takes you out, he'll be attentive, concerned about you, and generally a pretty nice person to be with. Then you meet one or two of his friends and suddenly your nice boyfriend becomes a prime candidate for the bad boy stakes.

He doesn't introduce you to anyone, he completely ignores you, he leaves you sitting on your own while he chats to his mates and he generally behaves as if you just don't exist.

He likes to feel free to chat up other girls at parties, to talk to his mates and generally to feel that he can do as he likes. At the same time, though, he likes the security of having a steady girlfriend. It's a classic case of the person who wants the best of both worlds.

The one thing in this bad boy's favour is that he won't actually two-time you and he'll be attentive and loving when

you're on your own. It's when other people are around that you'll suddenly become part of the wallpaper as far as he's concerned.

The last thing this boy wants is to be free. But he likes to play at being free. It's all a game, you see, and if you get entangled with this bad boy, you could end up the loser.

Falling for a genuine bad boy can be a heartbreaking experience and it can take a long time to recover.

Remember, though, the good guys really do outnumber the bad guys and chances are you'll be a whole lot luckier second time around!

Who Do You View?

Are you crazy about "Coronation Street," daft about "Dallas" and sold on "Superman"? If so, try our special TV and film quiz!

Cop That!

How much do you know about TV cops and robbers? Well, here's your chance to find out!

1. On which island does Jim Bergerac fight crime?

2. OK, so everyone knows they're called Cagney and Lacey. But what're their first names? Are they:
   a. Chris and Maggie,
   b. Maggie and Beth,
   c. Chris and Mary-Beth?

3. Which American police series does Tom Reilly star in?

4. General Lee is a bit of a fast character who is always being chased by the police. What show does he star in?

5. Lee Horsley stars as this Texas millionaire turned private eye. Can you name him?

6. Bodie and Doyle worked for C.I.5. in "The Professionals". What do these letters stand for?

Your Starter For Ten

Find out if you're our special "Mastermind" in this section on TV quizzes.

1. Dusty Bin stars in which quiz show?
2. Mike Read hosts which quiz show?
3. A computer called Mr Babbidge helps in this quiz show. Can you name it?

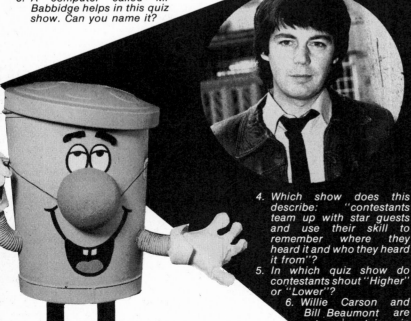

4. Which show does this describe: "contestants team up with star guests and use their skill to remember where they heard it and who they heard it from"?
5. In which quiz show do contestants shout "Higher" or "Lower"?
6. Willie Carson and Bill Beaumont are team captains in which quiz show?

Series Stuff

See how much you know about your favourite TV series.

1. Where do Petra Taylor, Gordon Collins and Roger Huntingdon all live?
2. Krystle, Fallon and Alexis star in which American series?
3. OK, "Fame" fans – everyone knows this is Carlo Imperato, but can you give us the full name of the character he plays in the series and what career he's aiming for?

4. He left school, where he had a reputation for being a real tearaway, and tried hard to get a job – who are we talking about?

5. Name the high-powered series this gorgeous guy appears in.
6. Name the dishy actor who stars as Brian Tilsley in "Coronation Street."

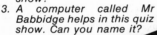

Music While You Watch

If you're a pop fan — then you're bound to do well with these questions on TV music programmes.

1. D.J. Peter Powell hosted this BBC 2 music show. Can you name it?
2. It began on January 1, 1964, and is Britain's longest-running pop programme. Name that show!
3. Lisa Stansfield jumped for joy when she was asked to present this mad-cap Tyne Tees show. What's it called?
4. This likely-looking lot starred in Channel 4's first Friday evening music show. Do you remember what it was called?
5. Unscramble these letters to discover a BBC 2 arts and music programme. VIREEDRSI
6. Name the show which combines a live pop concert with a simultaneous broadcast on Radio One.

2. This hunky heart-throb starred as Zak Mayo in a romantic movie. Two points if you can tell us the actor's name and also name the movie.
3. Which famous pop star played the lead role in "Merry Christmas, Mr Lawrence"?

4. Can you name Cannon and Ball's crazy comedy film?
5. What's special about "Jaws III"?
6. "Local Hero" was set in what part of Britain?
   a. Scotland.
   b. Wales.
   c. Northern Ireland.
7. OK, all you science-fiction fans. Name the third "Star Wars" movie.

Screen Test

Are you a film fan? Then try these movie questions for size!

1. What's the connection between Michael Jackson and E.T.? (No, it isn't that they're both out of this world!)

A Commercial Break

'Ad enough yet? No? Well try these questions!

1. What's "the best drink of the day"?
2. Barbara Woodhouse tells you to do what?
3. What's "tasty, tasty, very very tasty"?
4. What can you make someone happy with?
5. "If the name fits – wear it." What's the name?
6. "Bite it, crunch it, chew it." What are we talking about?

ANSWERS

Score one point for each correct answer.

Cop That!
1. Jersey 2. (c) 3. "C.H.i.P.s" 4. "The Dukes Of Hazzard" 5. "Matt Houston" 6. "Criminal Intelligence".

Your Starter For Ten
1. "3, 2, 1" 2. "Pop Quiz" 3. "Family Fortunes" 4. "Punchlines" 5. "Play Your Cards Right" 6. "A Question Of Sport".

Series Stuff
1. "Brookside" 2. "Dynasty" 3. Danny Amatullo — a comedian 4. Tucker Jenkins, alias actor Todd Carty 5. "Falcon Crest" 6. Christopher Quinten.

Screen Test
1. Michael collaborated on the "E.T. Storybook" album 2. Richard Gere — "An Officer And A Gentleman" 3. David Bowie 4. "Boys In Blue" 5. It's in 3-D 6. (a) 7. "Return Of The Jedi".

Music While You Watch
1. "The Oxford Road Show" 2. "Top Of The Pops" 3. "Razzmatazz" 4. "The Tube" 5. "Riverside" 6. "Sight And Sound In Concert".

A Commercial Break
1. Tea 2. "Go smash an egg!" 3. Kelloggs Bran Flakes 4. A phone call 5. Levi's 6. Lion Bar.

CONCLUSIONS

30-37 — Award yourself a pat on the back — you're definitely our media mastermind! There's not much you don't know about the world of TV and films. In fact, ignore everyone calling you "Square Eyes." We think they suit you!

20-29 — You're not exactly hooked on television and films but you have quite a good knowledge of them. You'll never threaten Barry Norman on "Film 83" or Barry Took on "Points Of View" but you're a normal Jackie TV and film fan.

19 and under — Mmm! D'you actually know what a TV is? It's that square thing that sits in the corner of your living-room — no, we're not speaking about your dad, stupid! As for the cinema, well, you probably don't even realise that the local flicks is now a bingo hall!

SWEET DREAMS!

Dreams may sometimes seem like jumbled nonsense or confused images in your mind, but in fact dreams and nightmares play a very important part in your life. Dreams hold the key to your secret self, so read on — and listen to your dreams!

Dreams Tell The Truth!

When you nod off into dreamland, your conscious mind may be taking a rest, but your subconscious mind's working overtime! It's working on your feelings and problems, passing messages from the deep, hidden part of your mind through to your conscious thoughts.

Imagine, for example, that you were walking to school deep in thought about this fella in your maths class that you fancy. You're in such a daze that you walk straight out into the road and a car misses you by inches. After the initial shock, you forget all about it, but that night you have a vivid dream . . . maybe it's more exaggerated than the actual incident — perhaps this time, the car really does hit you. On the other hand, the incident may creep into your dream in disguise — you may find yourself being chased by a bull, or falling from a cliff. Whichever form it takes,

though, this is a warning dream — warning you to keep your wits about you in future!

Who D'you Think You Are?

In the same way, dreams tell you what you really think of yourself — yes, they can see through your act and the image you like to portray! Say you like to come across as a life-and-soul type, bubbly, talkative and the centre of attention. Then along comes a nasty dream where you're standing in rags with crowds of people laughing at you — so what does this mean?

Your subconscious mind's telling you, through your dream, that you're not as confident as you like to think. It's telling you to come to terms with your feelings and be yourself — after all, putting on an act becomes pretty tiring after a while!

Of course, dreams can tell you nice things about yourself, too. For example, a hearts-and-flowers-crammed, romantic dream illustrates your soft, feminine side!

Nightmare Nasties!

We've all done it — woken up in a cold sweat, clutching our hot-water bottles in fear after a particularly nasty nightmare. Perhaps you've dreamed that someone you love has died or fallen ill, and the very fact that you could think such a thing really upsets you. Don't feel bad,